North Coast and Cascades Network Climate Monitoring Report

Olympic National Park; Water Year 2010

Natural Resource Data Series NPS/NCCN/NRDS—2012/262

William Baccus

National Park Service
North Coast and Cascades Network
Olympic National Park
600 E. Park Ave
Port Angeles, WA 98362

Mike Larrabee

National Park Service
North Coast and Cascades Network
North Cascades National Park Complex
810 State Route 20
Sedro-Woolley, WA 98284

Rebecca Lofgren and Mark Huff

National Park Service
North Coast and Cascades Network
Mount Rainier National Park
55210 238th Ave E.
Ashford, WA 98304

March 2012

U.S. Department of the Interior
National Park Service
Natural Resource Stewardship and Science
Fort Collins, Colorado

The National Park Service, Natural Resource Stewardship and Science office in Fort Collins, Colorado publishes a range of reports that address natural resource topics of interest and applicability to a broad audience in the National Park Service and others in natural resource management, including scientists, conservation and environmental constituencies, and the public.

The Natural Resource Data Series is intended for the timely release of basic data sets and data summaries. Care has been taken to assure accuracy of raw data values, but a thorough analysis and interpretation of the data has not been completed. Consequently, the initial analyses of data in this report are provisional and subject to change.

All manuscripts in the series receive the appropriate level of peer review to ensure that the information is scientifically credible, technically accurate, appropriately written for the intended audience, and designed and published in a professional manner. This report received informal peer review by subject-matter experts who were not directly involved in the collection, analysis, or reporting of the data. Data in this report were collected and analyzed using methods based on established, peer-reviewed protocols and were analyzed and interpreted within the guidelines of the protocols.

Views, statements, findings, conclusions, recommendations, and data in this report do not necessarily reflect views and policies of the National Park Service, U.S. Department of the Interior. Mention of trade names or commercial products does not constitute endorsement or recommendation for use by the U.S. Government.

This report is available from the Natural Resource Management Division at Olympic National Park, the North Coast and Cascades Network Inventory and Monitoring website (http://science.nature.nps.gov/im/units/nccn/reportpubs.cfm) and the Natural Resource Publications Management website (http://www.nature.nps.gov/publications/nrpm/).

Please cite this publication as:

Baccus, W. D., M. Larrabee, R. Lofgren, and M. Huff. 2012. North Coast and Cascades Network climate monitoring report: Olympic National Park; water year 2010. Natural Resource Data Series NPS/NCCN/NRDS—2012/262. National Park Service, Fort Collins, Colorado.

NPS 149/113090, March 2012

Contents

Figures

Figures (continued)

Figures (continued)

Figures (continued)

Tables

Appendices

Executive Summary

Climate and weather events define the ecological characteristics found in national parks and are key to understanding and interpreting changes in natural resources. Everyday park operations including; fire management, search and rescue, maintenance of park infrastructure, and visitor use are influenced by weather. Collecting weather data and maintaining climate records provides essential information needed to support park operations and to monitor park resources.

This report summarizes climate data collected in Olympic National Park during the 2010 water year, and is part of a set of climate summary reports from seven national and historic parks in the North Coast and Cascades Network. Published in the National Park Service's Natural Resource Data Series, annual climate summary reports are intended to provide basic data sets and data summaries in a timely manner, with minimal interpretation and analyses. We intend that the primary audience for this document will be National Park staff, especially decision makers, planners, and interpreters; partners; and interested public.

Temperature and precipitation data are presented from 11 weather stations ranging in location from the coast to high elevation sites in the mountainous core of the Olympics. Data were recorded using automated instruments operated by the National Park Service and other collaborators, including the National Weather Service and the Natural Resources Conservation Service. For two stations with long term records, the Quillayute Airport representing wet, west side conditions and the Elwha Ranger Station representing the drier, northern portions of the park, monthly average temperatures and monthly total precipitation are reported and compared to the 30-year normal (1971 to 2000). Monthly snow depth and snow water equivalent (SWE) are reported for two Snow Telemetry (SNOTEL) stations and three snow courses within the park.

Daily and monthly air temperature, precipitation and snowpack for the nine park operated weather stations are presented in individual appendices. Each appendix includes comparisons to the period of record, which varies by station. Highlights of important weather events and maintenance issues from each site are also noted.

Weather data collected in water year 2010 indicated that this year was generally cooler and wetter than normal. Of particular interest was a mid-season shift in weather, resulting in an unusually cold and wet spring and summer which contributed to delayed phenology and a prolonged mountain snowpack.

Acknowledgments

Olympic National Park relies on several cooperating agencies to help support and maintain a long-term climate monitoring program as part of the North Coast and Cascades (NCCN) climate monitoring program. These agencies include:

- Natural Resources Conservation Service - National Water and Climate Center, SNOTEL and Snow Survey Program

- National Weather Service – National Weather Service Cooperative Observer Program

- US Climate Reference Network, National Oceanic and Atmospheric Administration – National Climate Data Center.

- Northwest Weather and Avalanche Center – High Elevation Climate Stations

Data management is critical to provide for the availability and analysis of climate data. We depend on the NCCN Data Managers, specifically John Boetsch, Bret Christoe and Ruth Jenkins; the Western Regional Climate Center; and the National Climate Data Center for climate data management.

The authors appreciate the careful review by Catherine Copass, Janis Burger and Roger Hoffman. Finally, we thank the Office of the Washington State Climatologist and Dr. Cliff Mass (Weather Blog) for their regional and statewide weather and climate discussions.

Acronyms

COOP	Cooperative Observer Station
I&M	Inventory and Monitoring
NCCN	North Coast and Cascades Network
NCDC	National Climatic Data Center
NPS	National Park Service
NOAA	National Oceanic and Atmospheric Administration
NRCS	Natural Resources Conservation Service
NWAC	Northwest Weather and Avalanche Center
NWS	National Weather Service
OLYM	Olympic National Park
PNW	Pacific Northwest
SNOTEL	Snowpack Telemetry
SWE	Snow Water Equivalent
USDA	United States Department of Agriculture
WRCC	Western Regional Climate Center

Glossary

Climate Normals: A long-term average value of a meteorological parameter (i.e. temperature) measured at a specific station. For example, "temperatures are normal for this time of year" means that temperatures are at or near the average climatological value for a given time period. Climate normals are usually taken from data averaged over a 30-year period (e.g., 1971-2000), and are concerned with the distribution of data within limits of common occurrence.

Fall: The National Weather Service defines fall as the months of September, October and November.

NWS-COOP: An extensive network of manually operated weather stations overseen by the National Weather Service. Many Cooperative Observer Program weather sites were established in the late 1800's and as such, provide the best long term climate data. At each station, an observer records daily maximum and minimum temperature, as well as total rain and snowfall.

Period of Record: The total span of time that climate data have been collected at a specific location. The longer the period of record, the more likely the climate data will not be biased by singular weather events or cyclic climate anomalies such as those associated with the Pacific Decadal Oscillation and the El Niño/La Niña-Southern Oscillation.

RAWS: A network of Remote Automated Weather stations overseen by the National Interagency Fire Center. RAWS stations provide real-time weather data to assist land management agencies in monitoring fuels, rating fire danger and predicting fire behavior. RAWS stations all operate during summer months, and many at lower elevations operate on a year round basis.

SNOTEL: An automated network of snowpack data collection sites operated by the Natural Resources Conservation Service (NRCS). A standard SNOTEL station consists of a snow pillow, snow depth sensor, storage type precipitation gauge and air temperature sensor. Enhanced sites also measure soil moisture.

Snow Course: A permanent site where trained observers manually measure snow depth, snow water equivalent and density at a series of points along an established transect. Measurements are taken the last week of each month during winter and early spring. Values are recorded as the first of the month.

Snow Water Equivalent (SWE): A measurement describing the amount of water contained within the seasonal snowpack. It can be thought of as the depth of water that would theoretically result if you melted the entire snowpack instantaneously.

Spring: The National Weather Service defines spring as the months of March, April and May.

Summer: The National Weather Service defines summer as the months of June, July, and August.

Water Year: The Water Year (or Hydrologic Year) is most often defined as the period from October 1 to September 30 of the following year. It is called by the calendar year in which it ends. Thus, Water Year 2010 is the 12-month period beginning October 1, 2009 and ending September 30, 2010. The period is chosen so as to encompass a full cycle of precipitation accumulation.

Winter: The National Weather Service defines winter as the months of December, January and February.

Introduction

Climate is a dominant driver of the physical and ecologic processes of the North Coast and Cascades Inventory and Monitoring Network Parks (NCCN) (Davey et al. 2006). Trends in rainfall and temperature influence how an ecosystem and its organisms function. The quantity and timing of rainfall and snow can influence the productivity and health of forests (Nakawatase and Peterson, 2006), the amount of water flowing in streams and rivers (Hamlet, et al. 2007) and the growing or shrinking of mountain glaciers. Likewise, temperature can influence the quantity and timing of plant growth and stream runoff, or the extent and duration of winter snowpack and lake ice (Thompson et al. 2009). Through direct and indirect methods, climate affects the behavior and reproduction of terrestrial and aquatic animal species (Crozier et al. 2008). Climate is one of the primary causes of disturbance events such as forest fires (Littell and Gwozdz 2011), avalanches, windstorms, debris flows and floods. These events can have a major impact on park landscapes and their associated ecosystems as well as park infrastructure such as roads and campgrounds.

Given the importance of climate, it has been identified as a primary vital sign by all 32 Inventory and Monitoring (I&M) networks within the NPS (Gray 2008). The NCCN monitors climate in order to understand variations in other park resources being monitored; to compare current and historic data to understand long-term trends; and to provide data for modeling impacts to park facilities and resources in the future (Lofgren et al. 2010). Climate data, derived from the NCCN climate network will play an important role in understanding and interpreting the physical and ecological Vital Signs monitored within NCCN parks.

The NCCN climate monitoring program capitalizes on climate stations operated by partnering agencies, compiling data from over 60 weather stations in and adjacent to the parks, of which 15 are operated by the National Park Service. While a wide variety of climate parameters are measured as part of the NCCN climate program, this report focuses on two key parameters: precipitation and air temperature, while providing supplemental information on snowpack.

This report summarizes climate data collected from 11 weather stations located in and adjacent to Olympic National Park during the 2010 water year, and is part of a set of climate summary reports from seven national and historic parks in the NCCN (Figure 1). Temperature, precipitation, and snow data from the eleven weather stations are summarized in the results section of this report; and, detailed climate data recorded from each weather station are presented in Appendices A to I.

Annual climate summary reports are intended to provide basic data sets and data summaries in a timely manner, with minimal interpretation and analyses. National park staff, especially decision makers, planners, and resource educators; partners; and interested public are the primary audience.

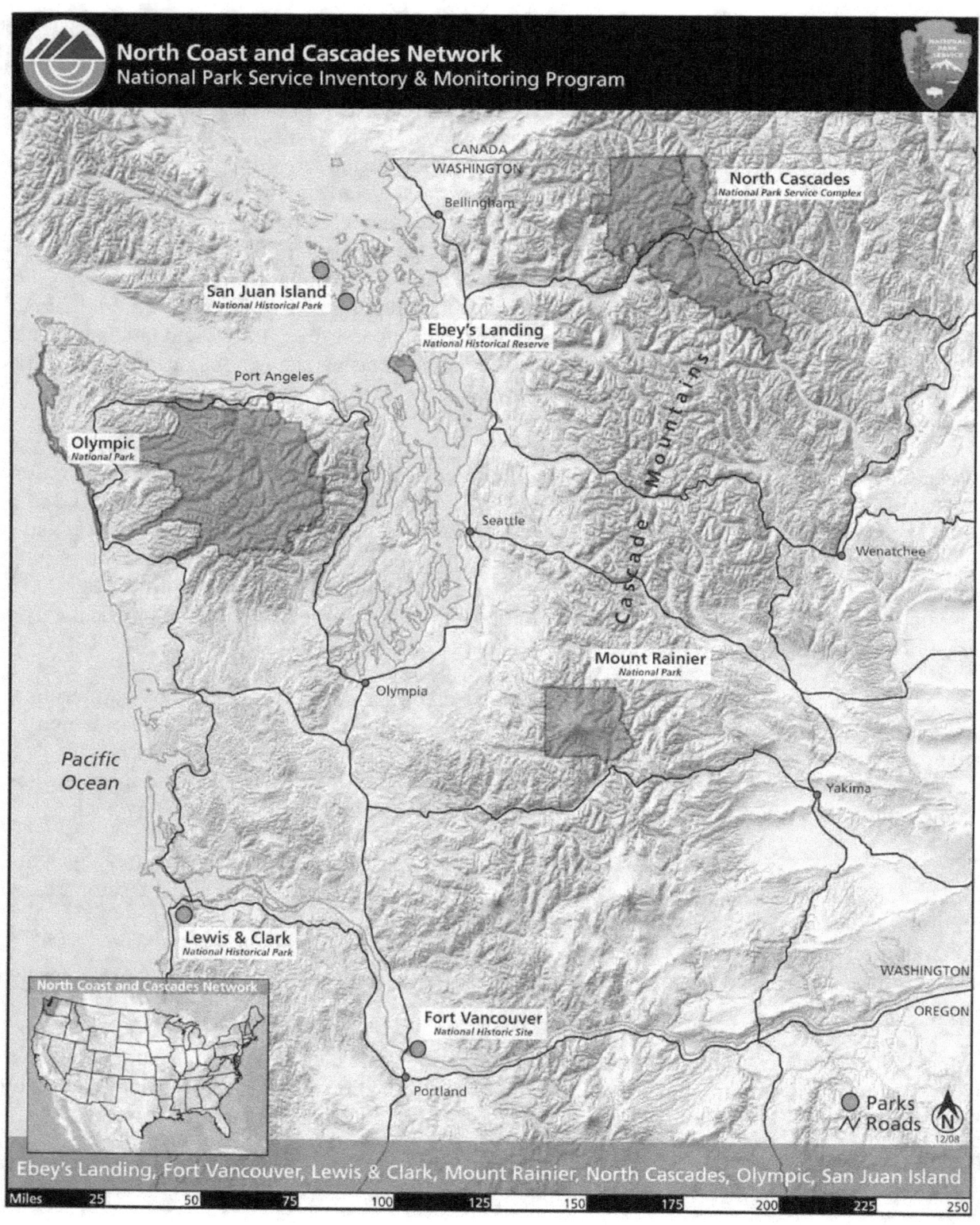

Figure 1. North Coast and Cascades Network Parks (NCCN).

Methods

Station Locations

This report incorporates data collected from weather stations operated by the NPS, the NRCS (SNOTEL), and the NWS (COOP) (Table 1 and Figure 2).

Table 1. Weather stations referenced in this report.

Station Name	Station Type	Location	Elevation (ft)	Forest Zone	Period of Record
Buckinghorse Ridge	SNOTEL	Interior	4870	Subalpine	2008 to Present
Deer Park Ranger Station	NPS	Northeast	5250	Subalpine	2007 to Present
Deer Park Road	NPS	Northeast	3115	Montane	1999 to Present
Elwha Ranger Station	COOP	North	390	Lowland	1942 to Present
Hayes River Guard Station	NPS	Interior	1700	Lowland	2007 to Present
Hoh Rainforest	NPS	West	406	Lowland	2000 to Present
Kalaloch Ranger Station	NPS	West	42	Coastal	1966[a] to Present
Ozette Ranger Station	NPS	Northwest	31	Coastal	2003 to Present
Quillayute Airport	COOP	West	180	Coastal	1966 to Present
Quinault Rainforest	NPS	Southwest	372	Lowland	1999 to Present
Waterhole	SNOTEL	North	4961	Subalpine	2000 to Present

[a] Annual precipitation values only. Hourly data from 2009 to present.

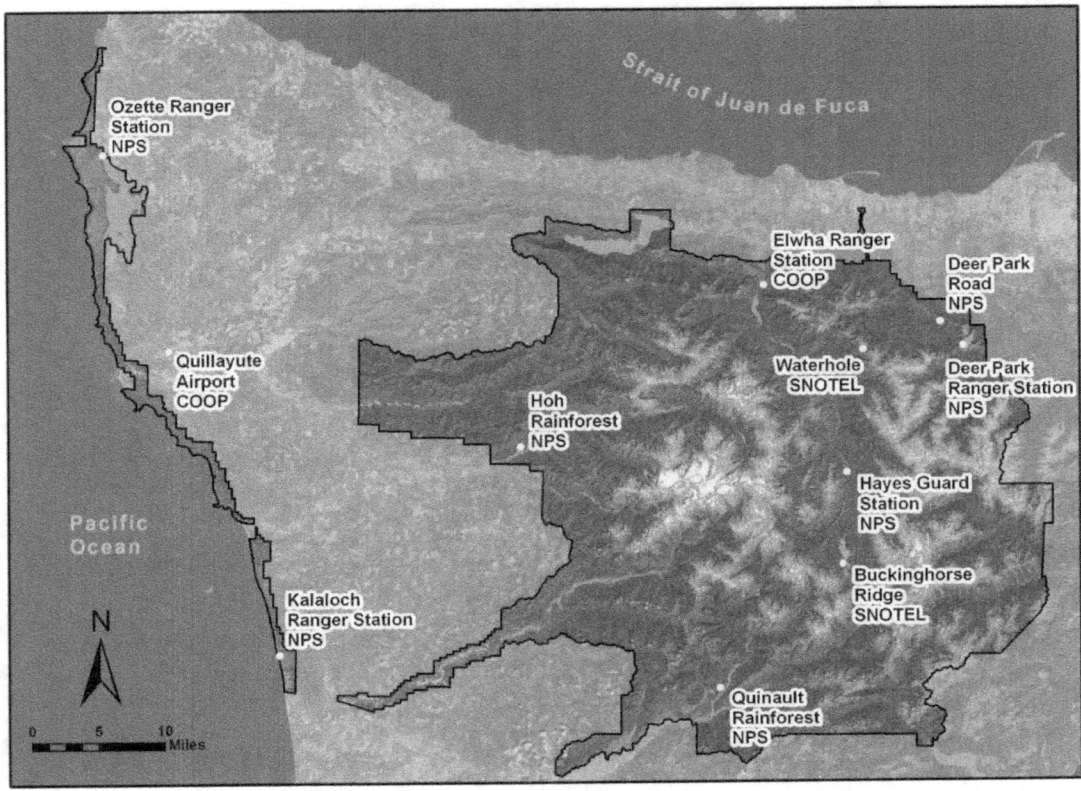

Figure 2. Location of weather stations referenced in this report.

Weather Station Measurements

Weather stations within the NCCN are managed by a variety of different agencies, each with a specific primary purpose. For this reason, instrumentation, method and period of collection may vary between sites. Table 2 describes the parameters measured at each station, highlights the data presented in this report, and indicates additional data that are available by request from Olympic National Park.

Table 2. Parameters measured at weather stations included in this report. **X** indicates the parameter is measured and data are presented in this report; x indicates parameter is measured and data are available on request.

Station Name	Managing Agency – Station Type	Air Temp	Relative Humidity	Precipitation	Snow Depth	Snowfall	Snow Water Equivalent	Solar Radiation	Photosynthetic Active Radiation	Wind Speed & Direction	Soil Temperature	Soil Moisture
Buckinghorse Ridge	SNOTEL[1]	X	x	X	X		X				x	x
Deer Park Ranger Station	NPS[2]	X	x	X	X							
Deer Park Road	NPS[2]	X	X	X					x	x	x	x
Elwha Ranger Station	NWS COOP[3]	X		X		x						
Hayes River Guard Station	NPS[2]	X	x	X	X						x	x
Hoh Rainforest	NPS[2]	X	x	X					x	x	x	x
Kalaloch Ranger Station	NPS[2]	X	x	X								
Ozette Ranger Station	NPS[2]	X	x	X				x		x		
Quillayute Airport	NWS COOP[3]	X		X		x						
Quinault Rainforest	NPS[2]	X	x	X					x	x	x	x
Waterhole	SNOTEL[1]	X	x	X	X		X				x	x

[1] SNOTEL utilize a standard array of automated weather instruments in support of water supply forecasting. Parameters are measured every 60 seconds, and output as hourly averages. These stations are managed and operated by the United States Department of Agriculture Natural Resource Conservation Service (USDA-NRCS)

[2] National Park Service (NPS) stations utilize a standard array of automated weather instruments which are measured at 5 minute intervals and output as hourly averages.

[3] National Weather Service Cooperative Stations (NWS COOP) stations rely on a standard array of manually operated weather instruments. Parameters are measured and recorded daily.

Data Quality

The weather station at the Deer Park Ranger Station was relocated during the summer of 2009 and became operational at the new site on October 11, 2009, leaving a gap in the data for the first ten days of the water year (See Appendix B). Power limitations restrict the use of a heated tipping bucket; therefore precipitation falling as snow cannot be accurately measured. Precipitation data for the months of November through March are not reported.

Summer air temperature data from the Kalaloch Ranger Station were omitted due to values appearing (5° to 10°F) lower than adjacent stations. This intermittent failure appears to relate to site-specific conditions adversely affecting the operation of the Vaisala HMP 45C temperature and relative humidity probe. Similar issues have been noted with these probes when operated at park rainforest research sites beneath the forest canopy that are exposed to prolonged periods of high humidity. This probe was replaced with a temperature thermistor probe in 2011.

A small amount of data is missing from the Ozette Ranger Station in December, May and June due to hardware-memory malfunctions. Missing precipitation data were replaced with precipitation values from the nearby Quillayute Airport. A new memory device was installed at this site in 2011.

In mid-October, a mechanical failure of the tipping bucket switch occurred at the Quinault Rainforest weather station located at Bunch Field. The tipping bucket was repaired in early July. Nine months of missing data were replaced using values from the Irely Lake research weather station, 2.75 miles northeast (up valley) of the Quinault Rainforest weather station.

Data Management

NWS COOP station and NRCS SNOTEL station data used in this report are acquired directly from the managing agencies. Quality assurance and control is provided by these agencies and is described in the NCCN Climate Monitoring Protocol (Lofgren et al. 2010).

The daily data used in this report from NPS and RAWS stations are derived from hourly data which have been evaluated through automated queries and manual display and graphing. Hourly data flagged or identified as suspect are omitted from daily summaries. If more than two hours of data are missing on a given day, no daily values are presented.

Monthly values are generated and presented for stations where five or fewer daily values are missing. In the case of missing precipitation values, daily quantities may be substituted from another nearby weather station for the purposes of reporting monthly and annual totals. This will only occur when nearby data are available and a known correlation exists between these sites. In these cases where estimates are generated from nearby stations, data are footnoted and a description of the quantity and source of data replacement is given.

Data Reporting

Data in this report are based on the hydrologic or water year and organized by month and seasons. Ecosystems in the Pacific Northwest are dominated by two distinct hydrological periods, a wet season generally beginning in late October and ending in June, and a drought season that generally extends from July to September. While a calendar year divides the wet winter season, the use of a water year closely reflects the timing and seasonality of many physical and ecological processes that are driven by climate, such as soil saturation and forest evapotranspiration, onset and breakup of lake ice, glacial accumulation and ablation balances, the magnitude and timing of stream flow, emergence and flowering of plants and the migratory timing of bird species.

Seasons in this report are distinguished based on National Weather Service (NWS) standards for the Northern Hemisphere. The NWS defines December, January, and February as winter; March, April, and May as spring; June, July, and August as summer; and September, October, and November as fall.

The main report provides monthly averages of daily average temperatures and monthly total precipitation for all stations listed in Table 2. While routinely collected in metric units, the data are presented in Fahrenheit and inches to more easily facilitate use and interpretation by park staff and the public. Two stations with long term records: the Quillayute Airport representing wet, west side conditions and the Elwha Ranger Station representing the drier, northern portions of the park are compared to the 30-year climate normal. Snow water equivalent is reported and compared to the 30-year climate normal for one SNOTEL and three snow courses within the park.

The appendices are divided by individual climate station and present daily data for precipitation, temperature, and snowfall or snow water equivalent when available, as well as average, maximum, minimum temperatures and total precipitation for each month. While the main report compares Water Year 2010 with the 30-year climate normal, the appendices compare 2010 with the period of record for that station. Detailed discussion of maintenance issues or data concerns associated with each specific station is also presented.

Results

Temperature

Near normal temperatures were observed in October and November at all stations (Table 3; Figures 4 and 5). Temperatures were colder than normal during the month of December before an extended period of above normal temperatures from January to late March. The Quillayute Airport recorded the second warmest January on record, a departure of +5.7°F (Figure 4). In late March, a marked shift to a cooler weather pattern began and continued into early summer. Late spring and early summer temperatures averaged 1.0°F below normal (Figures 4 and 5). The cooler temperatures were apparent in delayed spring phenology of many tree species and a late ice-out of mountain lakes (Figure 3). July and August temperatures continued to be below normal at nearly all weather stations. The exceptions were lower elevation sites in the northeast portion of the park. The Elwha Ranger Station (Figure 4) and the mid-elevation station on the Deer Park Road (see Appendix C) both recorded at or slightly above normal temperatures during this period. In contrast, the Quillayute Airport on the west side of the Olympic Peninsula recorded below normal temperatures during summer months. This discrepancy is likely due to a persistent fog and a marine layer which blanketed coastal and lowland areas of the Peninsula throughout much of the summer. A University of Washington researcher determined 2010 as the foggiest in the last 44 years (Johnstone 2011).

Figure 3. Heavy snow still covers Hoh Lake and the surrounding basin on June 22, 2010. Due to the deep snowpack and below normal spring and summer temperatures, the lake would not thaw until July 20 2010, several weeks later than normal.

Table 3. Average monthly air temperatures (°F) from weather stations within or adjacent to Olympic National Park in Water Year 2010.

Season	Month & Year	Buckinghorse Ridge SNOTEL	Deer Park Ranger Station	Deer Park Road	Elwha Ranger Station COOP	Hayes River Guard Station	Hoh Rainforest	Kalaloch Ranger Station	Ozette Ranger Station	Quillayute Field COOP	Quinault Rainforest	Waterhole SNOTEL
Fall	October 2009	39.0	---[1]	45.2	48.7	42.7	45.5	50.1	50.1	49.7	49.2	35.4
	November 2009	33.2	28.4	38.7	41.0	36.6	42.4	45.9	46.9	45.3	41.0	29.2
Winter	December 2009	29.7	23.8	33.2	33.7	29.1	34.1	37.6	37.3	38.6	33.8	24.0
	January 2010	34.6	29.6	39.8	41.1	37.8	43.7	47.3	45.8	46.3	45.4	30.9
	February 2010	33.8	29.8	39.3	42.1	37.0	42.3	45.4	45.2	45.6	43.2	29.6
Spring	March 2010	33.2	28.6	38.1	43.7	36.6	42.3	45.0	44.6	45.1	43.2	29.1
	April 2010	33.7	29.8	39.3	46.5	39.2	43.9	46.4	46.7	46.7	45.1	28.8
	May 2010	37.8	33.8	43.8	50.6	44.9	47.6	48.7	---[2]	48.8	49.5	34.6
Summer	June 2010	44.3	40.6	47.9	54.5	52.2	53.2	49.9	---[2]	54.2	55.6	41.3
	July 2010	54.8	52.5	60.8	61.6	59.9	58.3	---[3]	56.3	57.7	60.5	51.5
	August 2010	54.7	51.6	60.1	62.1	58.6	58.0	---[3]	56.7	58.4	60.8	51.7
Fall	September 2010	47.0	44.9	52.6	55.8	52.2	55.1	---[3]	56.7	57.7	58.2	45.4
	Water Year	39.7	---[1]	44.9	48.5	43.9	47.2	---[3]	---[2]	49.5	48.8	36.0

[1] Eleven days of temperature data missing due to a datalogger failure.

[2] Ten days of temperature data are missing in May and 15 days in June due to a memory malfunctions on the datalogger.

[3] Air temperature data are missing due to the failure of the air temperature sensor in early July.

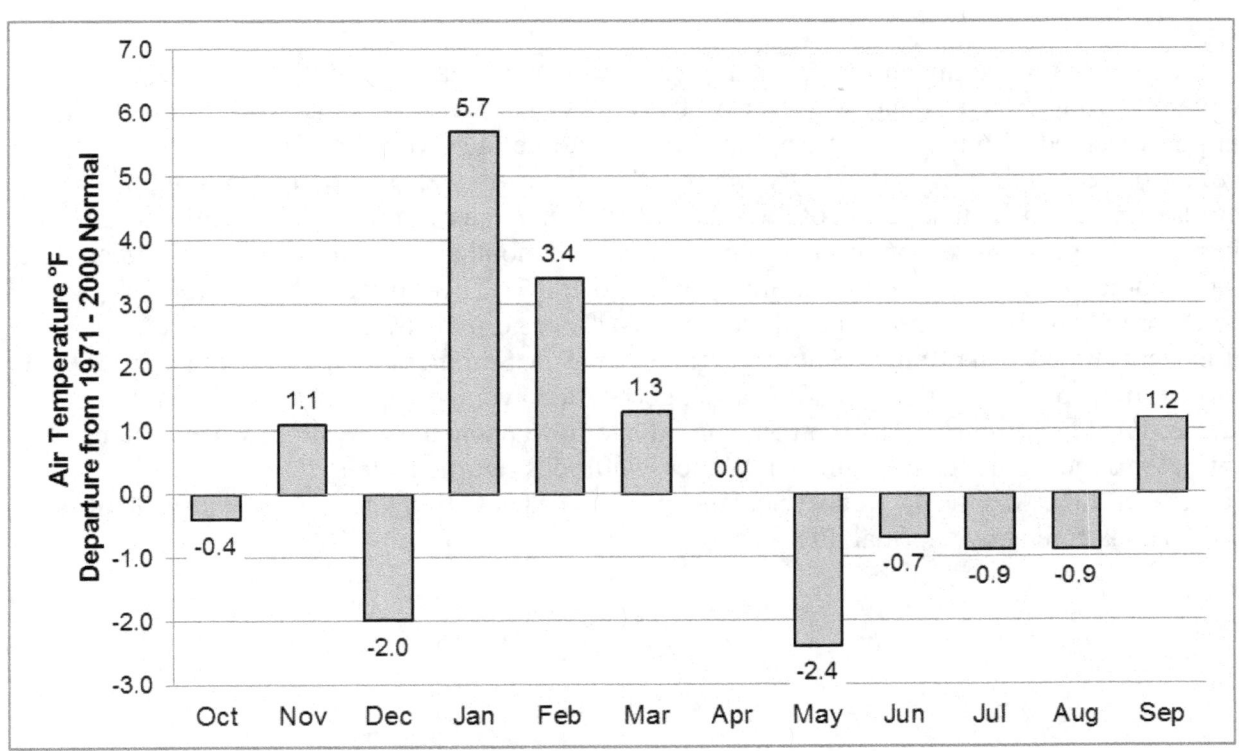

Figure 4. Comparison of average monthly temperature (°F) for Quillayute Airport in Water Year 2010 against monthly averages for the climatological normal 1971-2000.

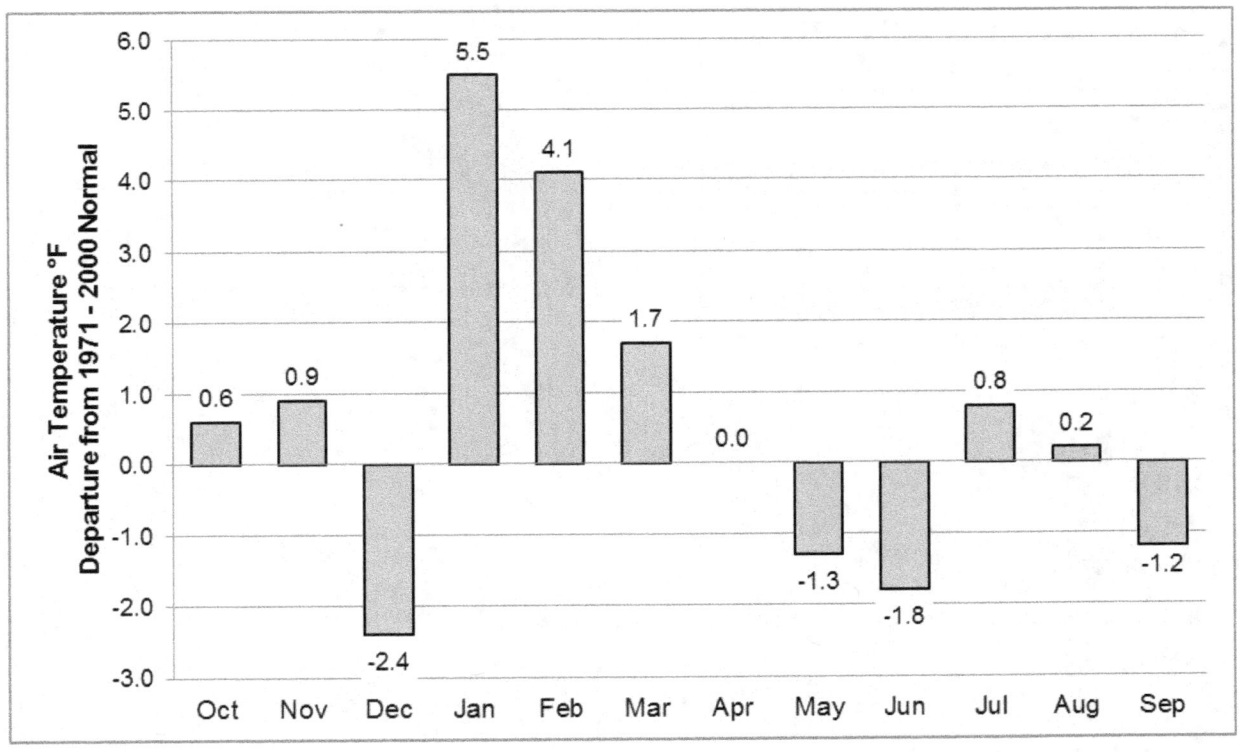

Figure 5. Comparison of average monthly temperature (°F) for Elwha Ranger Station in Water Year 2010 against monthly averages for the climatological normal 1971-2000.

Precipitation

Fall months exhibited higher than normal precipitation at all stations, continuing a trend from September (unpublished data, Water Year 2009). November was particularly wet. The Quillayute Airport received 26.6 inches of precipitation in the month of November (Table 4), the second wettest on record for this traditionally wet month and the 4th wettest month ever at the Quillayute station (with a period of record of 43 years). Winter months were slightly drier than normal (-15% departure from normal), however spring months resumed the trend of higher than normal precipitation (52% above normal) (Figure 6 and 7). The month with the largest departure from normal was May, when precipitation was 147% of normal at Quillayute Airport and 273% of normal at the Elwha Ranger Station (Figures 6 and 7). Summer months were much drier than normal in the park's interior. The Elwha Ranger Station averaged only 24% of normal for June, July and August (Figure 7). In contrast, coastal and lowland areas were slightly wetter than normal in June and August (Figure 6). Wetter conditions returned late in the water year. September 2010 was the 4th wettest September on record at Quillayute station, with 8.9" of rain (214% departure above normal, Figure 6).

Table 4. Total monthly precipitation (inches) from weather stations within or adjacent to OLYM in Water Year 2010.

Season	Month & Year	Buckinghorse Ridge SNOTEL	Deer Park Ranger Station	Deer Park Road	Elwha Ranger Station COOP	Hayes River Guard Station	Hoh Rainforest	Kalaloch Ranger Station	Ozette Ranger Station	Quillayute Field COOP	Quinault Rainforest	Waterhole SNOTEL
Fall	October 2009	18.9	5.6	5.3	7.7	10.9	15.2	12.4	12.0	12.3	18.4	9.7
	November 2009	39.1	----[a]	12.3	18.8	26.3	32.6	24.8	24.4	26.6	33.6	23.5
Winter	December 2009	10.7	----[a]	3.3	4.6	6.6	8.5	5.5	7.5[c]	6.9	8.9	5.9
	January 2010	27.4	----[a]	7.9	12.3[b]	17.1	21.3	15.9	16.5	22.5	21.9	15.7
	February 2010	12.2	----[a]	1.7	3.6[b]	6.5	9.4	7.7	6.8	7.2	11.8	4.1
Spring	March 2010	14.1	----[a]	3.0	6.1[b]	8.7	12.1	9.2	8.9	9.8	10.5	8.9
	April 2010	13.7	2.4	2.4	5.3[b]	7.4	13.3	9.5	8.6	10.1	12.8	7.5
	May 2010	9.0	4.1	3.4	5.3	6.2	9.9	8.2	7.6[c]	8.1	7.8	6.2
Summer	June 2010	2.3	0.9	1.1	0.7	1.1	2.6	4.2	4.3[c]	4.3	2.5	1.0
	July 2010	0.3	0.3	0.3	0.1	0.2	0.3	0.4	0.5	0.4	0.4	0.1
	August 2010	1.6	0.3	0.3	0.1	0.5	2.3	3.6	3.2	2.9	1.2	0.8
Fall	September 2010	7.8	2.0	2.3	3.1	4.2	7.1	7.3	6.7	8.9	7.4	2.8
	Water Year 2010	157.1	-----	43.3	67.7	95.7	134.6	108.7	107.0	120.0	137.2	86.2

[a] Non-heated tipping bucket. No winter values available.

[b] Values for the months of January, February, March and April are missing greater than 5 days of precipitation.

[c] Values for eight days in December,19 days in May and 15 days in June were estimated from the Quillayute Airport COOP due to data loss at the Ozette Weather Station.

11

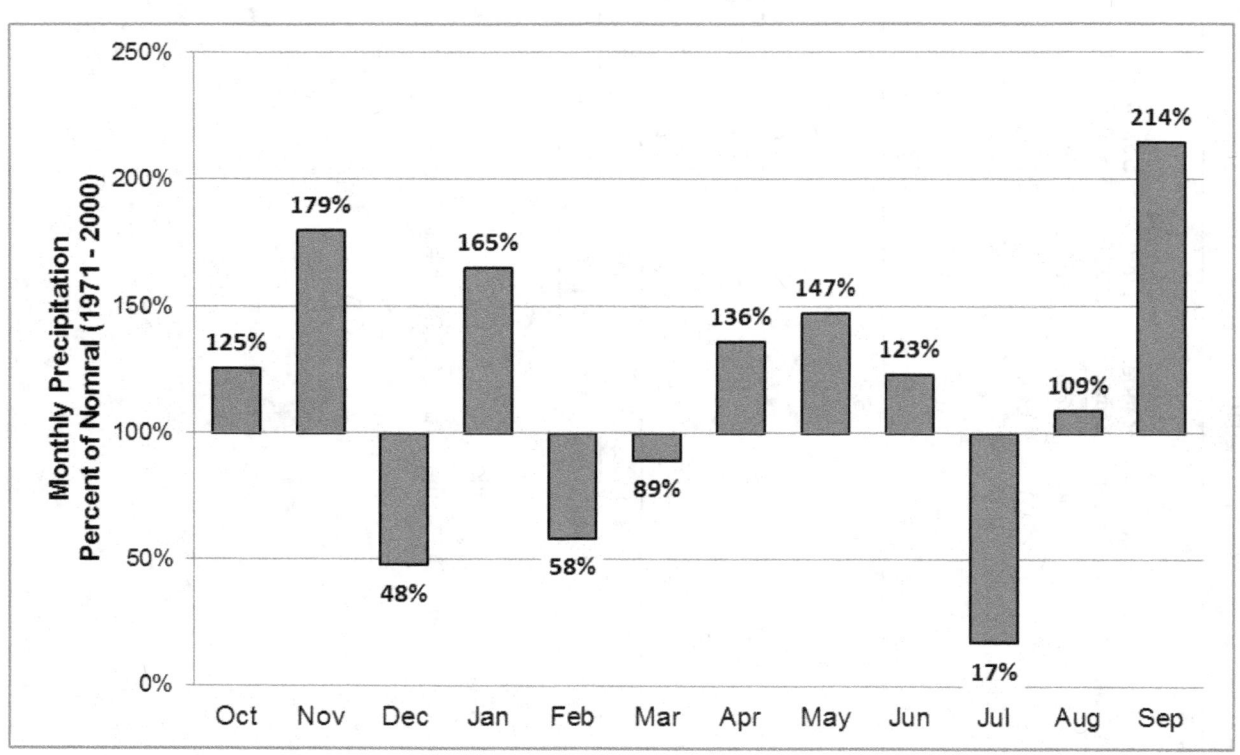

Figure 6. Comparison of total monthly precipitation (inches) at Quillayute Airport in Water Year 2010 against the climatological normal 1971-2000.

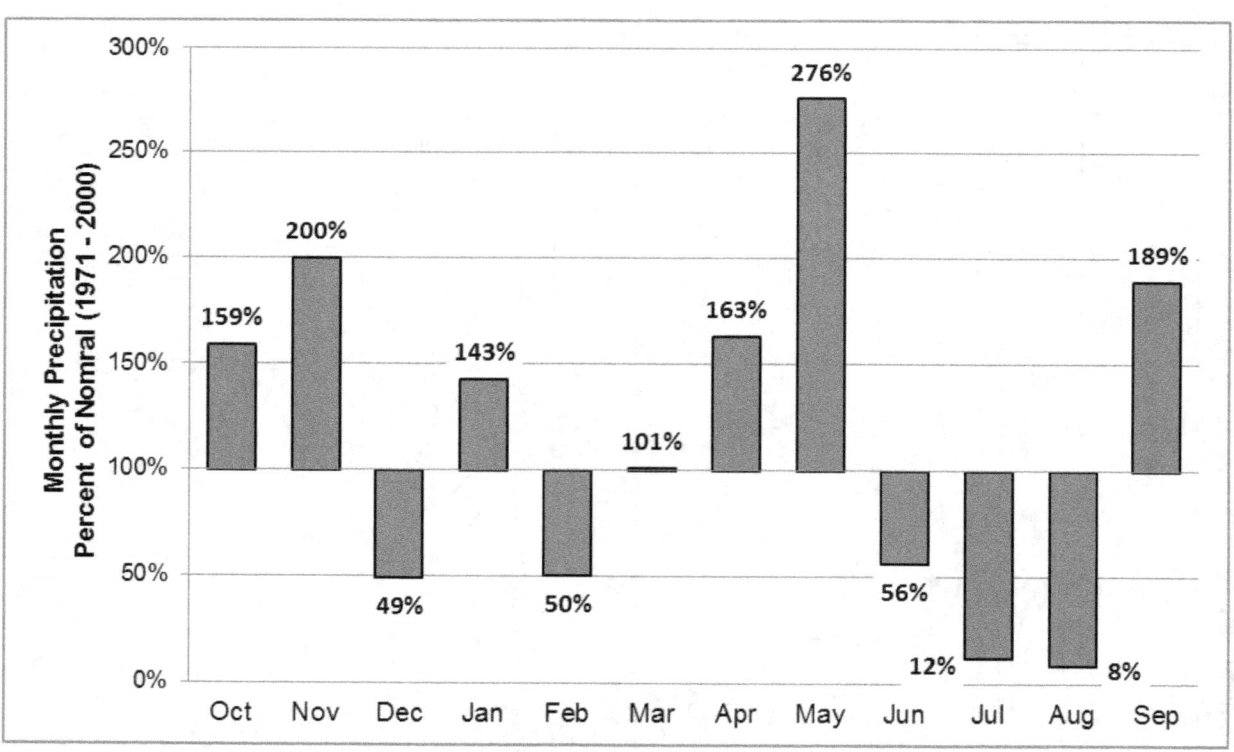

Figure 7. Comparison of total monthly precipitation (inches) at the Elwha Ranger Station in Water Year 2010 against the climatological normal 1971-2000.

Snow

Despite above normal temperatures in the fall and winter, record breaking precipitation associated with a series of winter storms created an unusually deep early season snowpack. On December 1, the Waterhole SNOTEL had 47 inches of snow and a 17 inch snow water equivalent (333% greater than normal, Table 5, Figure 9 and Appendix I). Limited snowfall during the warmer than normal winter months (Figure 5), slowed the rate of snow accumulation and the snowpack was near normal through the end of March (Figures 8, 9, 10, 11 and 12). Cold and wetter than normal conditions during April and May preserved and further built the snowpack. By June 1, the Waterhole SNOTEL was 73% greater than normal (Figure 9).

Table 5. Snow Depth (inches) measured on the first day of the month at SNOTEL and snow courses within Olympic National Park during Water Year 2010.

Month & Year	Buckinghorse Ridge SNOTEL	Waterhole SNOTEL	Cox Valley Snow Course	Deer Park Snow Course	Hurricane Snow Course
November 1st 2009	0.0	0.0			
December 1st 2009	76.0	47.0			
January 1st 2010	78.0	51.0			
February 1st 2010	108.0	68.0	64.9	36.2	24.1
March 1st 2010	131.0	75.0	63.4	35.4	22.4
April 1st 2010	165.0	106.0	101.6	52.1	54.0
May 1st 2010	158.0	97.0	88.0	45.3	36.2
June 1st 2010	137.0	81.0			
July 1st 2010	72.0	15.0			

Figure 8. View south from the Deer Park Snow Course on March 1, 2010. Warm temperatures during the previous two months had reduced the snow pack to 85% of normal. This condition would change dramatically by the next month's snow survey.

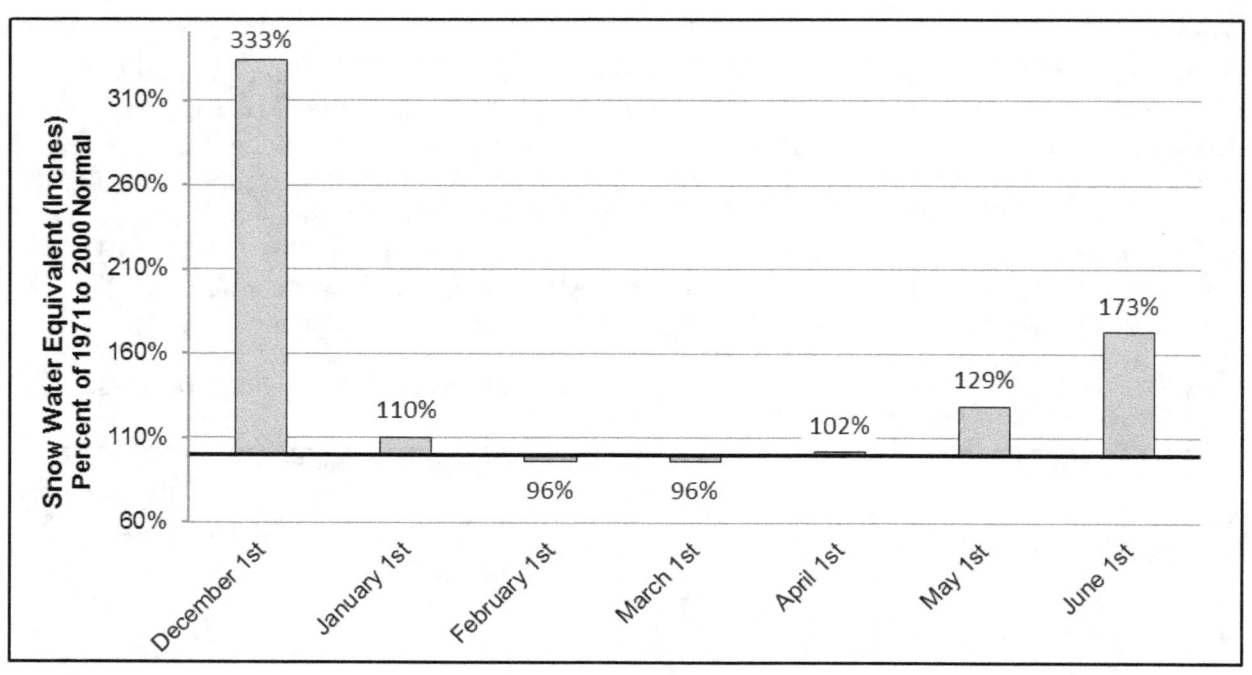

Figure 9. Comparison of snow water equivalent (inches) at the Waterhole SNOTEL in Water Year 2010 against the climatological normal 1971-2000.

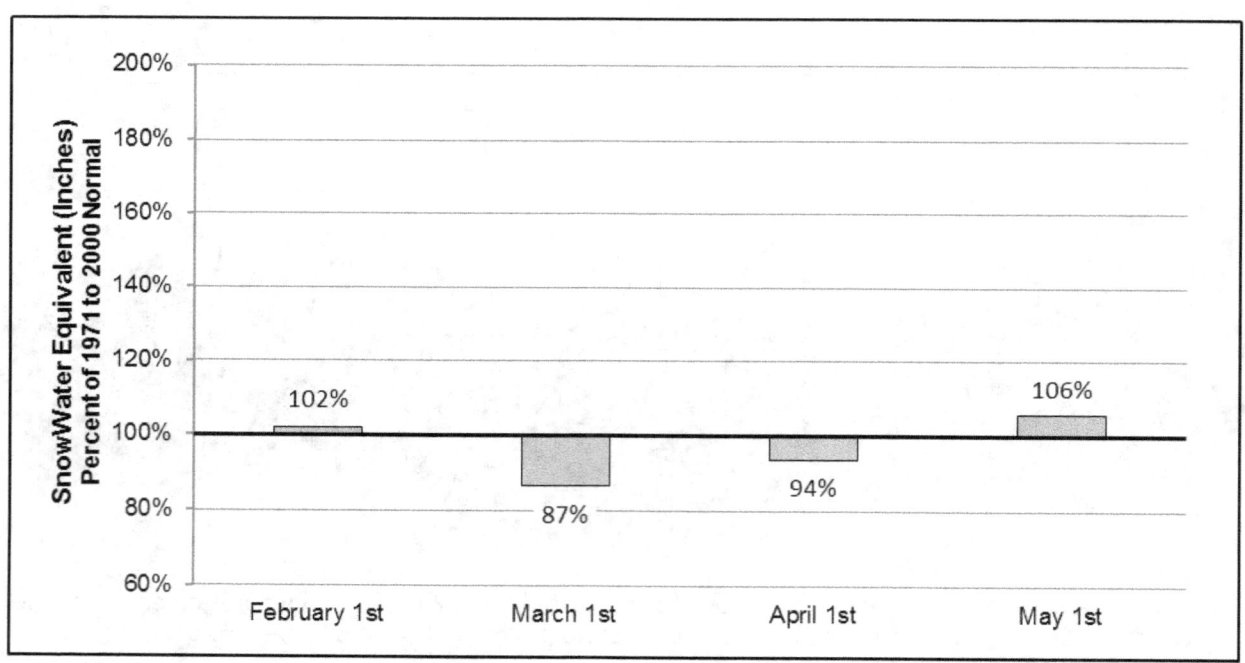

Figure 10. Comparison of snow water equivalent (inches) at the Cox Valley Snow Course in Water Year 2010 against the climatological normal 1971-2000.

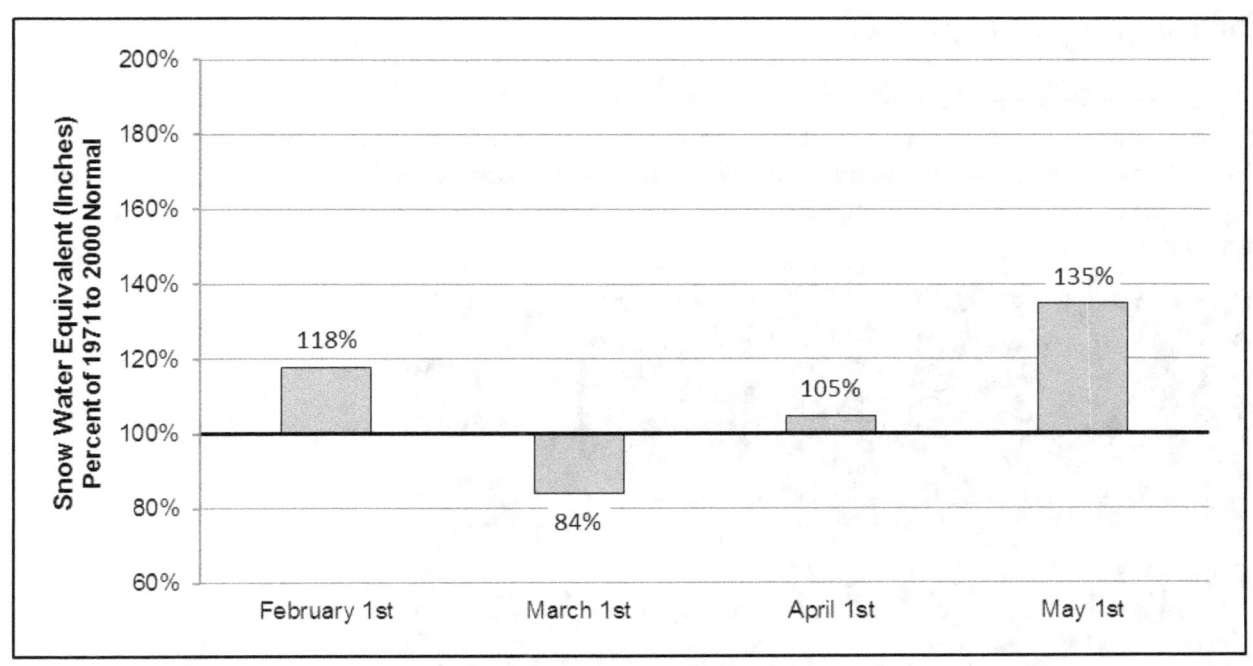

Figure 11. Comparison of snow water equivalent (inches) at the Deer Park Snow Course in Water Year 2010 against the climatological normal 1971-2000.

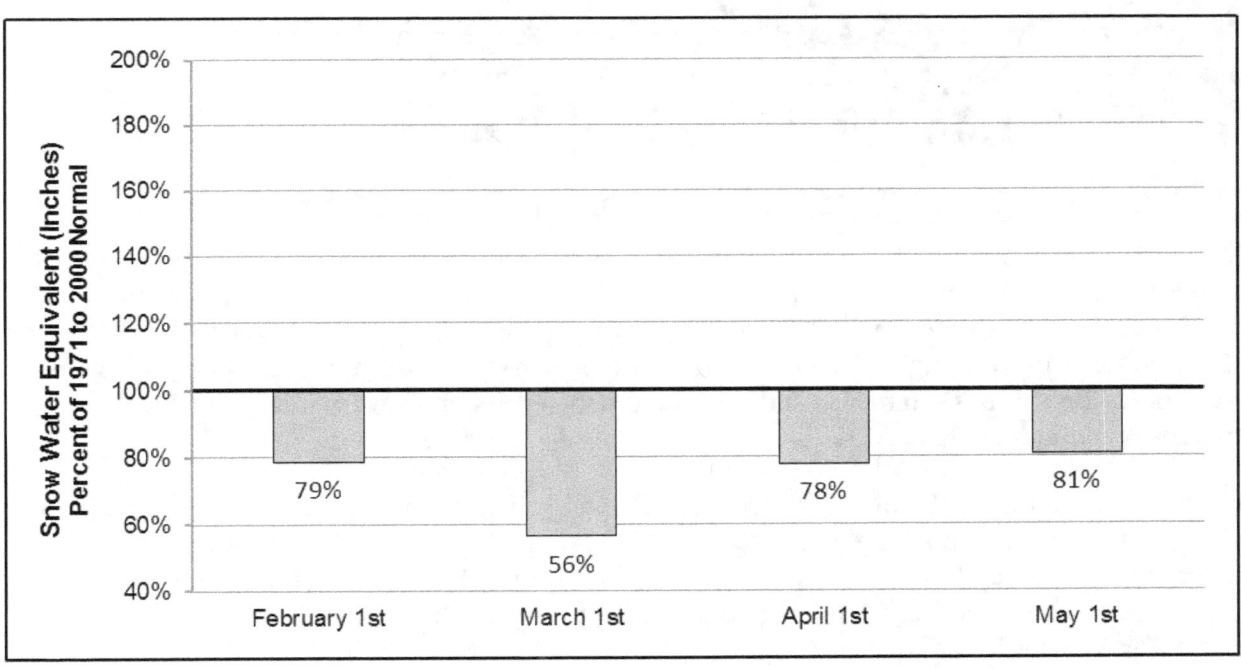

Figure 12. Comparison of snow water equivalent (inches) at the Hurricane Snow Course in Water Year 2010 against the climatological normal 1971-2000.

2010 Water Year in Review

Significant Weather Events

Several major winter storms in mid-November saturated lowlands and blanketed the Olympic Mountains with an early season snowpack. Amidst these storms, major wind events impacted the west side of the park on November 17 and 18. Hurricane Ridge recorded maximum winds of 78 miles per hour.

Figure 13. Slope failure destroyed the Hurricane Ridge Road in early January, 2010.

December was generally dry and cold with little snow accumulation in the mountains. A series of warm, wet storms beginning on January 11 caused minor flooding on the Olympic Peninsula and contributed to a mudslide which destroyed a portion of the Hurricane Ridge Road just below Heart of the Hills. The highest winds of the year (87 mph) were recorded on January 18. January was one of the warmest on record and combined with a dry February to limit growth of the snowpack in the mountains.

In late March, a major climatic shift occurred. Winter storms pummeled the Olympics on March 28, 29, and April 2, depositing large amounts of snow and creating minor flooding and wind damage in the lowlands. Winter-like weather continued into May. Heavy snow fell in the Olympic Mountains on May 2 and 3, and a windstorm struck the park on May 19 when winds of 83mph were recorded at Hurricane Ridge.

The summer months of June, July and August were generally cool and wet, especially at lower elevations and in those areas on the west side of the Olympic Peninsula affected by a persistent marine layer of clouds. The cold temperatures in June and July preserved the mountain snowpack, contributing to late melt out of mountain lakes and meadows, and high flows on rivers well into early July. Summer ended early with a wetter than normal September.

Parkwide Precipitation Summary

The southwestern slopes of the Olympic Mountains receive among the highest precipitation in the United States. Precipitation at four park weather stations exceeded 100 inches for the 2010 water year, with the highest amount occurring at the Buckinghorse Ridge SNOTEL, 157.1 inches (Figure 14). With a dramatic mountain-rainshadow effect on the Olympic Peninsula from southwest to northeast, precipitation at the Elwha Ranger Station COOP and Deer Park Road weather stations was two to three times lower than stations on the southwest-side (Figure 14).

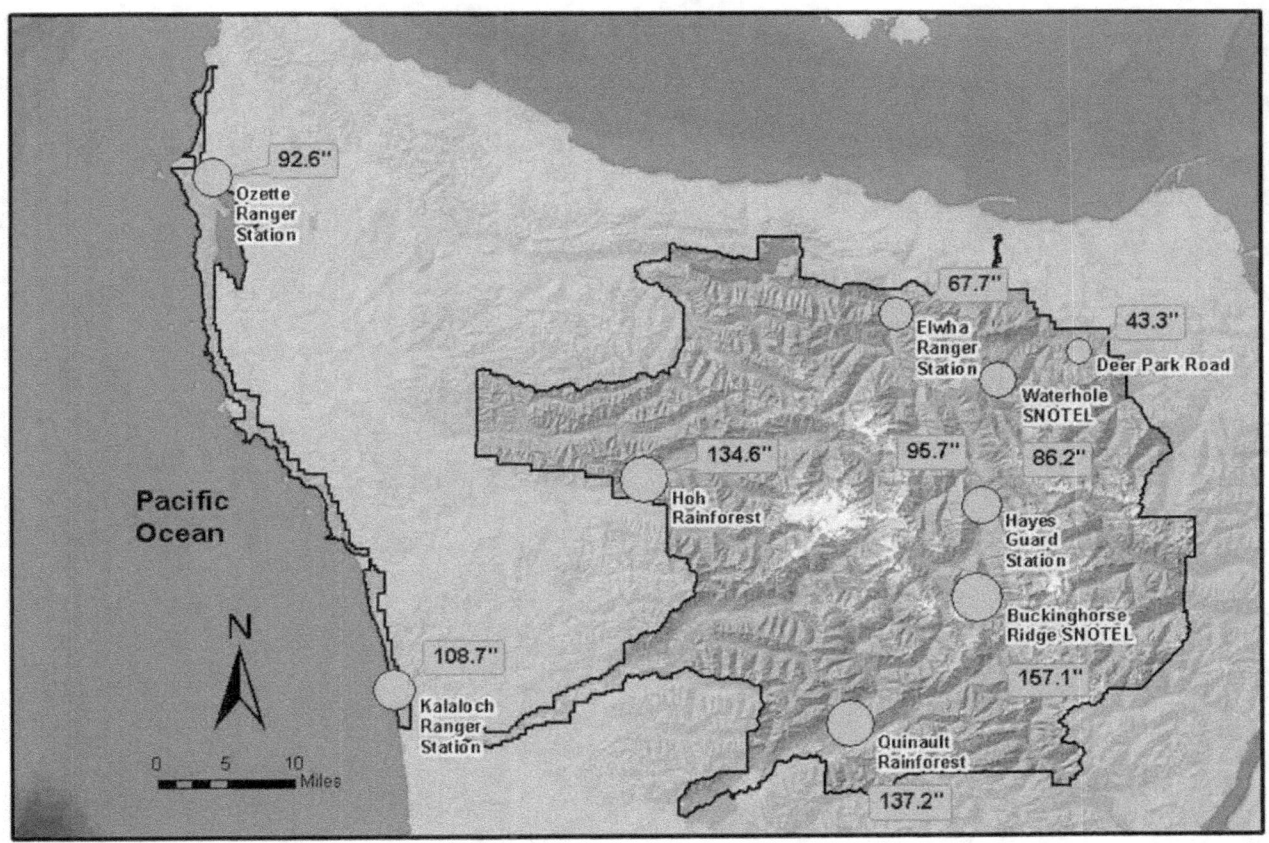

Figure 14. Total precipitation measured at weather stations located within Olympic National Park during Water Year 2010. Blue circles are proportional to the total amount of precipitation measured at each site.

Literature Cited

Crozier, L. G., A. P. Hendry, P. W. Lawson, T. P. Quinn, N. J. Mantua, J. Battin, R. G. Shaw, and R. B. Huey. 2008. Potential responses to climate change in organisms with complex life histories: Evolution and plasticity in Pacific salmon. Evolutionary Applications 1(2):252–270, doi:10.1111/j.1752-4571.2008.00033.x.

Davey, C. A., K. T. Redmond, D. B. Simeral. 2006. Weather and climate inventory National Park Service North Coast and Cascades Network. Natural Resource Technical Report NPS/NCCN/NRTR—2006/010. National Park Service, Fort Collins, Colorado. Available online: https://irma.nps.gov/Reference.mvc/DownloadDigitalFile?code=147109&file=2006_10_23_nccninventory_final.pdf (accessed 5 December 2011).

Gray, S. 2008. Framework for linking climate, resource inventories and ecosystem monitoring. Natural Resource Technical Report NPS/GRYN/NRTR-2008/110. National Park Service, Fort Collins, Colorado.

Hamlet, A. F., P. W. Mote, M. P. Clark, and D. P. Lettenmaier. 2007. 20th century trends in runoff, evapotranspiration, and soil moisture in the Western U.S. Journal of Climate 20(8):1468-1486. DOI: 10.1175/JCLI4051.1.

Johnstone, J. 2011. A review of a 'San Francisco Summer' for the Pacific Northwest. Presentation at the Pacific Northwest Weather Workshop, 2011. Website http://www.wrh.noaa.gov/sew/2011pnwww/Johnstone.pdf (accessed 24 October 2011).

Littell, J. S., and R. Gwozdz. 2011. Climatic water balance and regional fire years in the Pacific Northwest, USA: Linking regional climate and fire at landscape scales. Chapter 5, pp. 117-139 in D. McKenzie, C. M. Miller, and D. A. Falk (eds.). The Landscape Ecology of Fire, Ecological Studies 213, Springer, Dordrecht, The Netherlands, doi 10.1007/978-94-007-0301-8_5.

Lofgren, R., B. Samora, B. Baccus, and B. Christoe. 2010. Climate monitoring protocol for the North Coast and Cascades Network (Mount Rainier National Park, Olympic National Park, North Cascades National Park, Lewis and Clark National Historical Park, Ebey's Landing National Historical Reserve, San Juan Islands National Historical Park, Fort Vancouver National Historic Site): volume 1. narrative and appendices,version 5/26/2010. Natural Resource Report NPS/NCCN/NRR—2010/240. National Park Service, Fort Collins, Colorado.

Mantua, N. 2010. The Joint Institute for the Study of the Atmosphere and Oceans, University of Washington. *The Pacific Decadal Oscillation* website. http://www.atmos.washington.edu/~mantua/REPORTS/PDO/PDO_egec.htm (accessed 2 November 2011).

Nakawatase, J. M, and D. L. Peterson. 2006. Spatial variability in forest growth – climate relationships in the Olympic Mountains, Washington. Canadian Journal of Forest Resources 36:77–91.

Redmond, K. 1998. Western Regional Climate Center, Desert Research Institute. *El Niño, La Nina, and the Western U.S., Alaska and Hawaii Frequently Asked Questions* website. http://www.wrcc.dri.edu/enso/ensofaq.html (accessed 30 March 2011).

Thompson, R., M. Ventura, and L. Camarero. 2009. On the climate and weather of mountain and sub-arctic lakes in Europe and their susceptibility to future climate change. Freshwater Biology 54:2433-2451.

Appendix A: Buckinghorse Ridge SNOTEL - Water Year 2010

This was the first complete year of operation for the Buckinghorse SNOTEL. The site was installed in September 2008 but was disabled during August and September 2009 due to a forest fire in the vicinity of the equipment. Due to the recent installation of this site, no period of record comparisons can be made.

Temperatures ranged from an extreme low of 5.5°F during a particularly cold period in mid-December, to a maximum of 77.9°F in mid-August (Table A-1). Several extensive periods of above freezing temperatures are apparent in January and an unusual and prolonged period of below freezing temperatures were recorded in late March and early April (Figure A-1).

The Buckinghorse SNOTEL, with 157.1 inches of total precipitation, was the wettest station in the park during 2010 (Table 4). This site also had the highest monthly precipitation, with 39.1 inches of precipitation during the month of November (Figure A-2). Notable high daily precipitation fell between November 15 and 17, and during a "pineapple express" storm event on January 11 (Figure A-3).

Snowpack began developing on November 6, 2009 and melted July 25, 2010. The snowpack persisted for 262 days. Maximum snowpack occurred on April 9, with a depth of 182 inches and a SWE of 75.7 inches (Figure A-4).

Table A-1. Monthly summary data, Buckinghorse Ridge SNOTEL, Water Year 2010.

Season	Month & Year	Mean Air Temp °F	Max Daily Air Temp °F	Min Daily Air Temp °F	Precipitation (inches)
Fall	October 2009	39.0	57.6	27.3	18.9
	November 2009	33.2	53.4	18.5	39.1
Winter	December 2009	29.7	56.5[b]	5.5	10.7
	January 2010	34.6	46.2	23.0	27.4
	February 2010	33.8	47.8	23.7	12.2
Spring	March 2010	33.2	50.9	18.5	14.1
	April 2010	33.7	53.6	17.1	13.7
	May 2010	37.8	57.4	21.4	9.0
Summer	June 2010	44.3	63.1	30.4	2.3
	July 2010	54.8	75.7	31.1	0.3
	August 2010	54.7	77.9	36.1	1.6
Fall	September 2010	47.0	68.2	34.7	7.8
Water Year Total		39.7	77.9	5.5	157.1

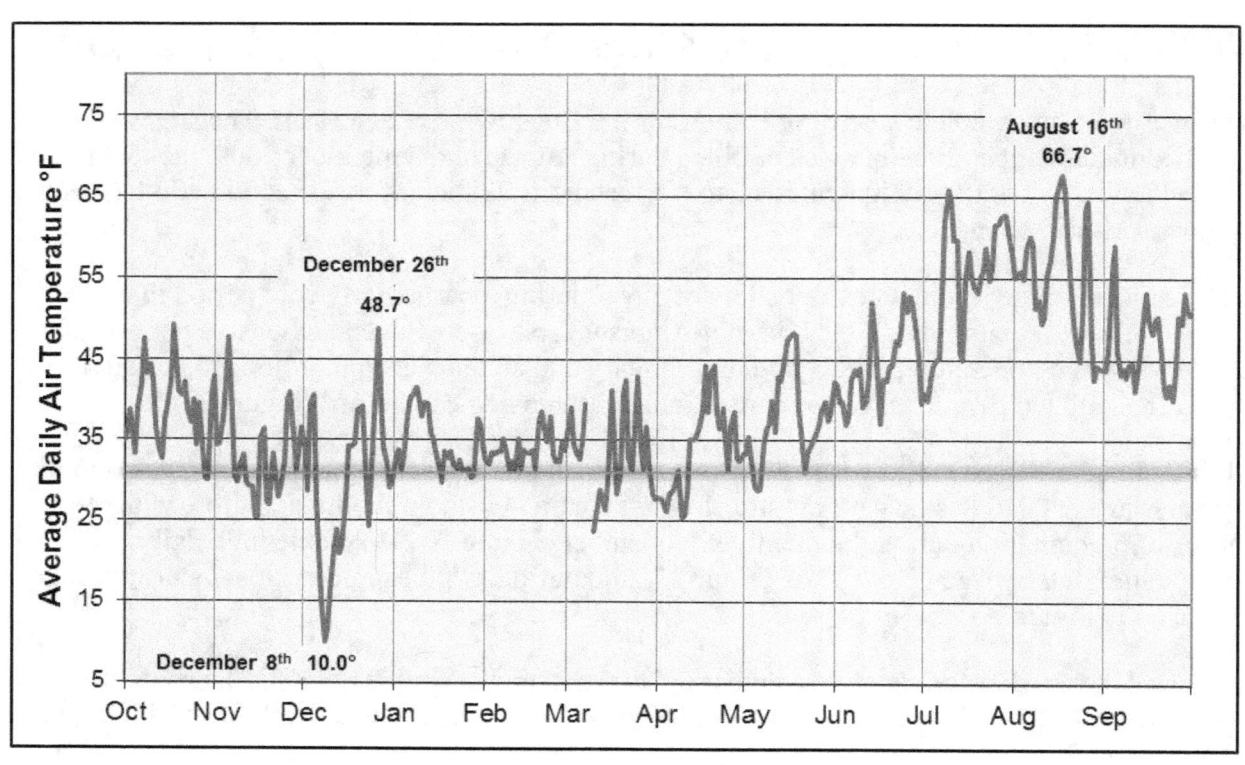

Figure A-1. Daily average air temp (°F) at Buckinghorse Ridge SNOTEL, Water Year 2010. Blue line indicates 32ºF, the freezing point of water.

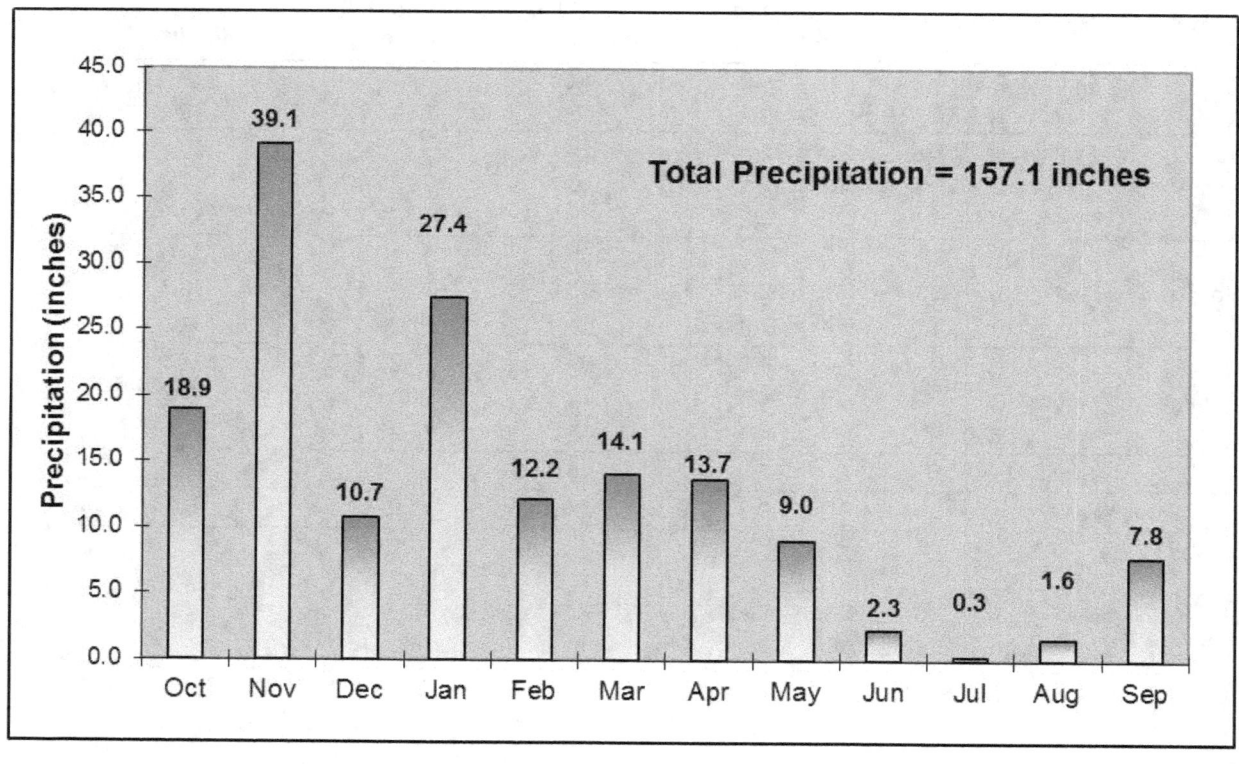

Figure A-2. Monthly precipitation values at Buckinghorse Ridge SNOTEL, Water Year 2010.

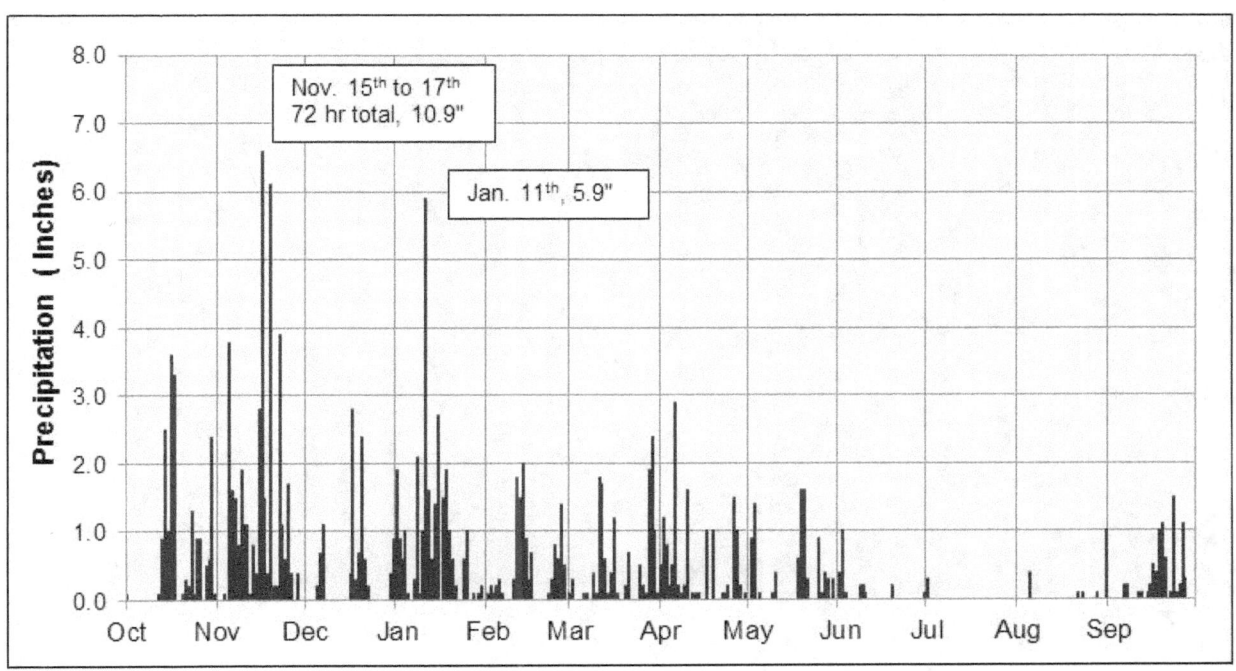

Figure A-3. Daily precipitation (inches) at Buckinghorse Ridge SNOTEL, Water Year 2010.

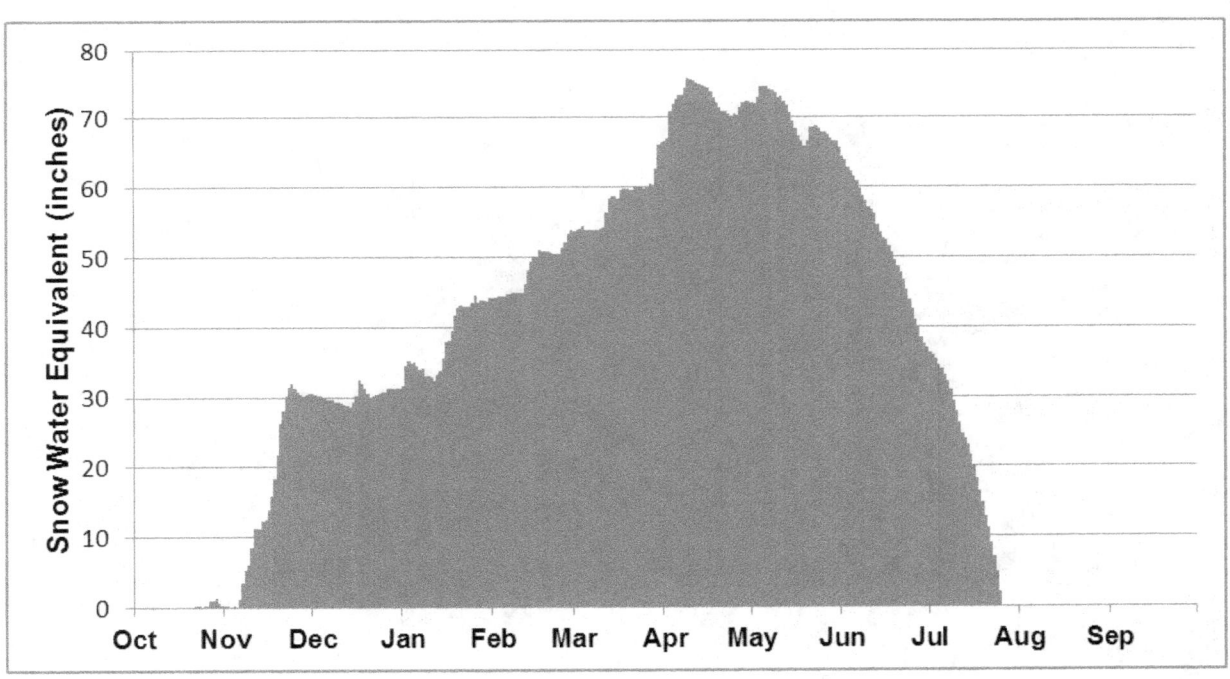

Figure A-4. Daily snow water equivalent (SWE) at Buckinghorse Ridge SNOTEL, Water Year 2010.

Appendix B: Deer Park Ranger Station - Water Year 2010.

In late June of 2009, the weather station was moved from its original location adjacent to the Deer Park Ranger Station, to a new location 0.25 mile east (Figure B-1). The new site occupies a small forested clearing on the same series of level terraces where the historic snow course occurs. The original site did not replicate snow conditions found on the snow course and was subject to snow drift and wind. The new site better meets the criteria for collecting precipitation

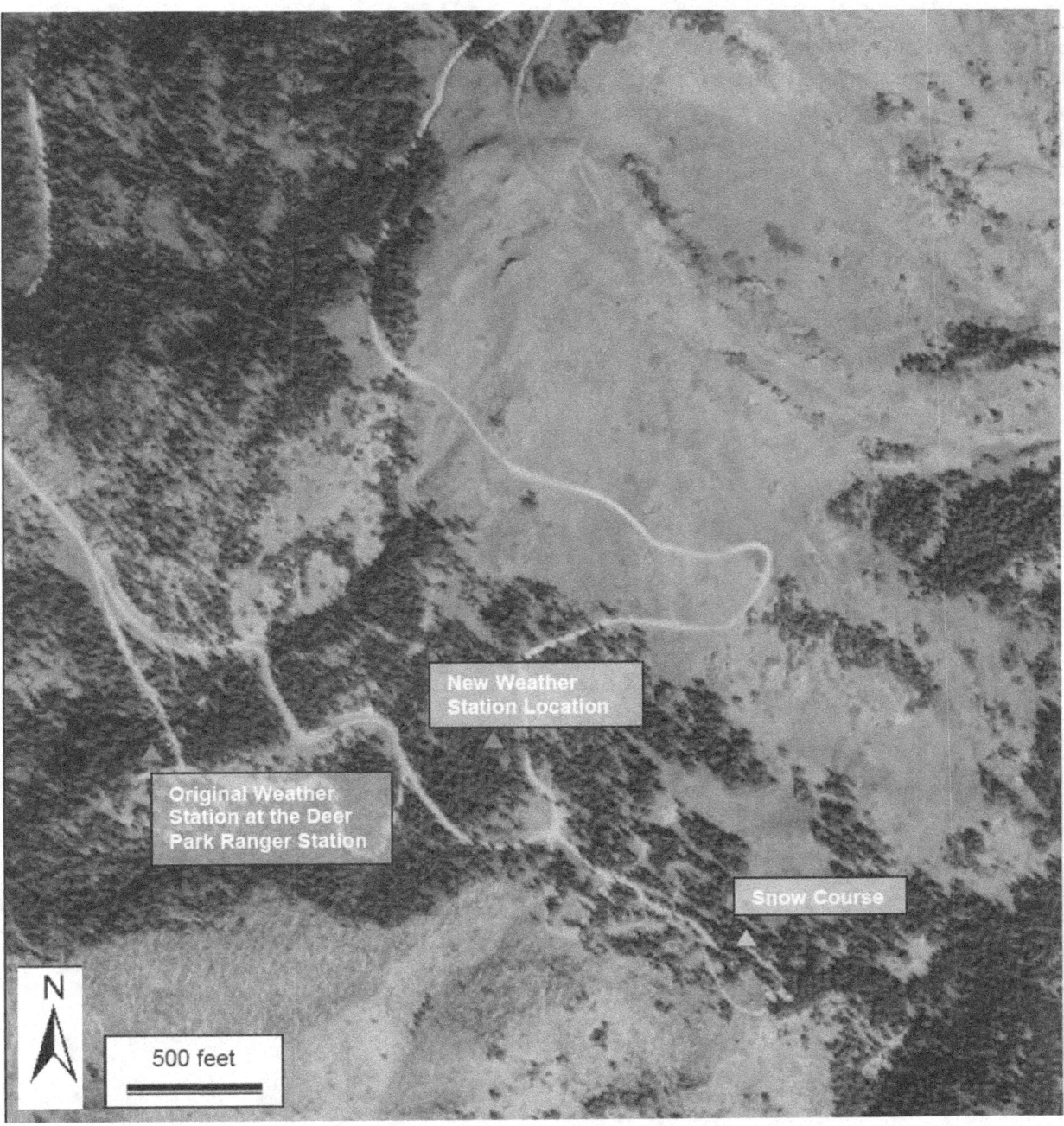

Figure B-1. Map showing the new location of the Deer Park Ranger Station weather station.

and limiting snow drift. The weather station became operational at the new site on October 11, leaving a gap in the data for the first ten days of the water year.

Daily air temperatures ranged from an extreme low of -0.9°F during a particularly cold period in mid-December, to a maximum of 77.7°F in mid-August (Table B-1). Several prolonged periods of below freezing temperatures are noteworthy in mid-December and again during the early parts of both April and May (Figure B-2). A high precipitation event was noted on October 18, when 2.8 inches of rain was recording in a 48 hour period (Figure B-4).

Snowpack began developing on November 6, 2009 and melted on the June 17, 2010. The snowpack persisted for 227 days. Maximum snow depth was 84.7 inches on April 2, 2010 (Figure B-4). Snowpack in the early season was near the average, decreased to below average during the dry and warmer period of mid-winter, then rebounded to just above average due to cold and snowy conditions in the months of April and May (Figure B-5).

Table B-1. Monthly summary data, Deer Park Ranger Station, Water Year 2010.

Season	Month & Year	Mean Air Temp °F	Max Daily Air Temp °F	Min Daily Air Temp °F	Precipitation (inches)
Fall	October 2009	---- [a]	---- [a]	---- [a]	5.6 [b]
	November 2009	28.4	54.7	9.2	---- [c]
Winter	December 2009	23.8	53.4	-0.9	---- [c]
	January 2010	29.6	42.8	15.6	---- [c]
	February 2010	29.8	48.0	17.3	---- [c]
Spring	March 2010	28.6	52.7	10.0	---- [c]
	April 2010	29.8	55.0	10.6	2.4
	May 2010	33.8	54.2	13.0	4.1
Summer	June 2010	40.6	61.6	25.3	0.9
	July 2010	52.5	74.6	30.2	0.3
	August 2010	51.6	77.7	29.6	0.3
Fall	September 2010	44.9	69.8	29.4	2.0
Water Year Total		**35.8**	**77.7**	**-0.9**	---- [c]

[a] Ten days of missing data in October. No method of estimating or interpolating data.

[b] Ten days of missing data in October. Precipitation data for this period was interpolated from Deer Park Road weather station.

[c] Non-heated rain gauge underestimates precipitation amounts during snow dominated periods.

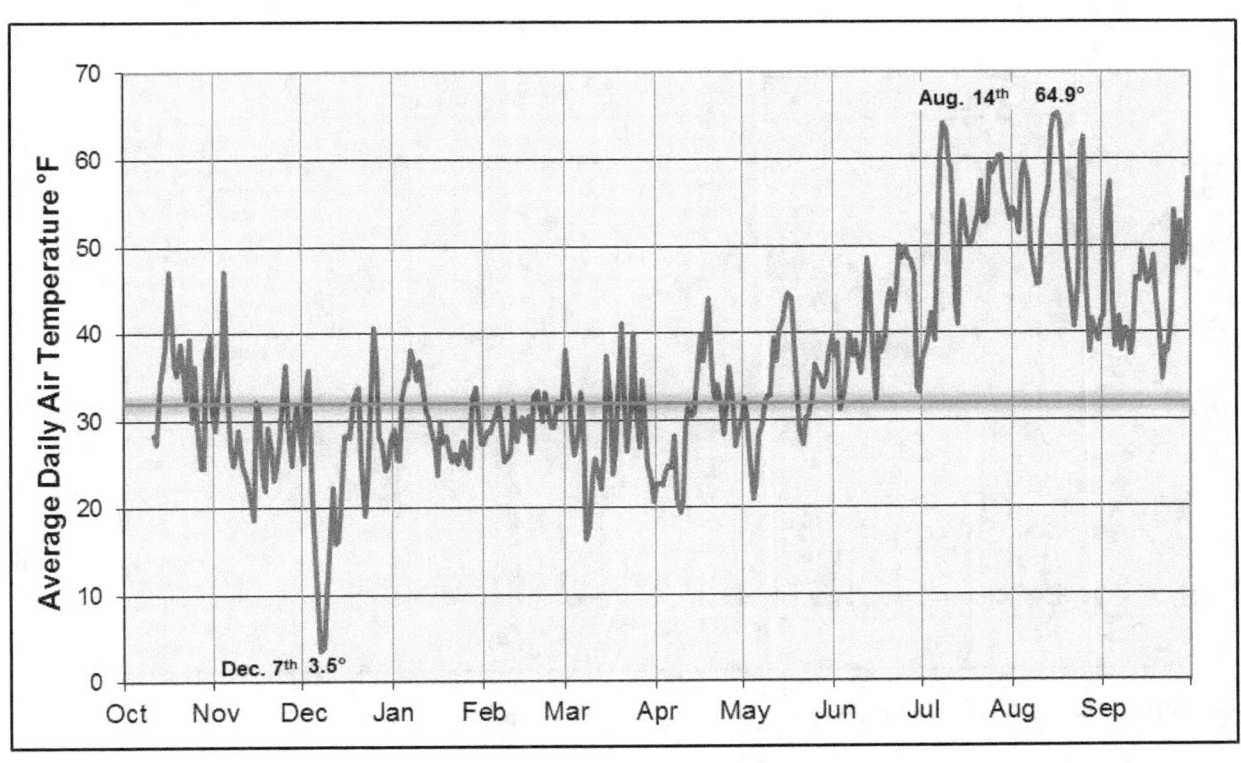

Figure B-2. Daily average air temp (°F) at Deer Park Ranger Station, Water Year 2010. Blue line indicates 32°F, the freezing point of water.

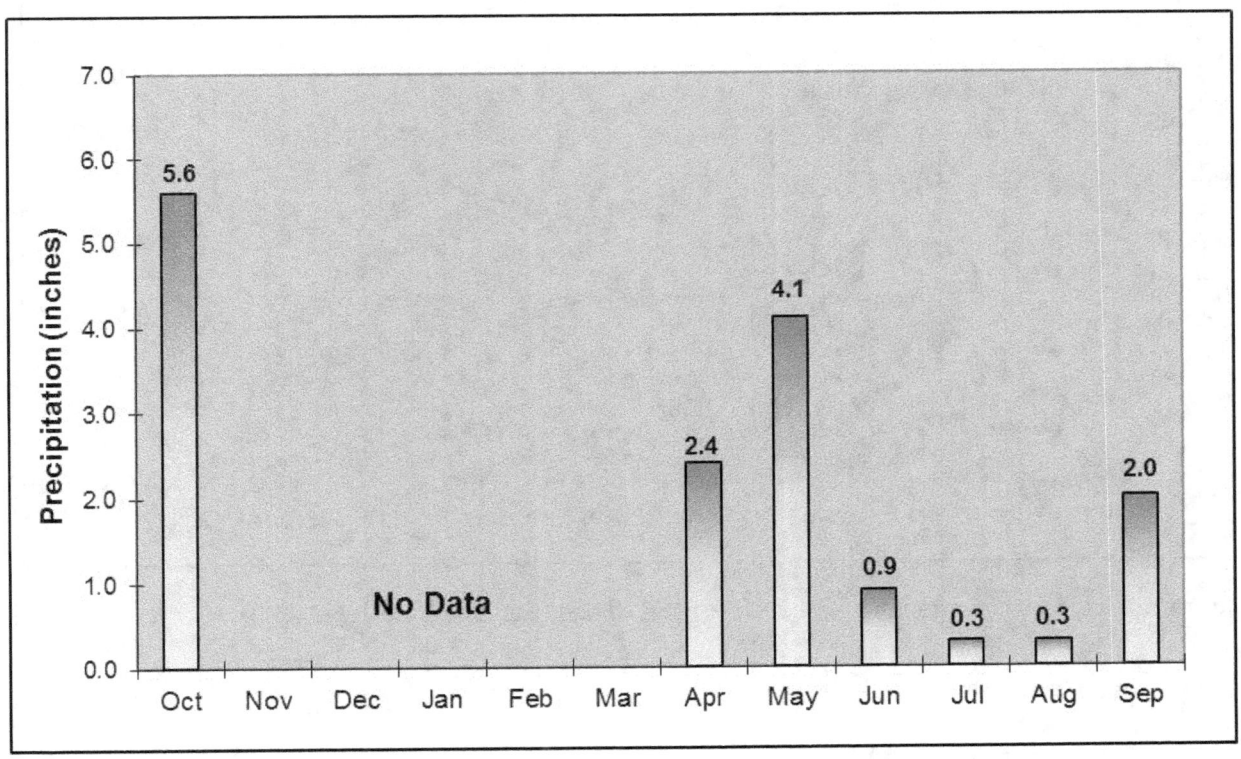

Figure B-3. Monthly precipitation values at Deer Park Ranger Station, Water Year 2010.

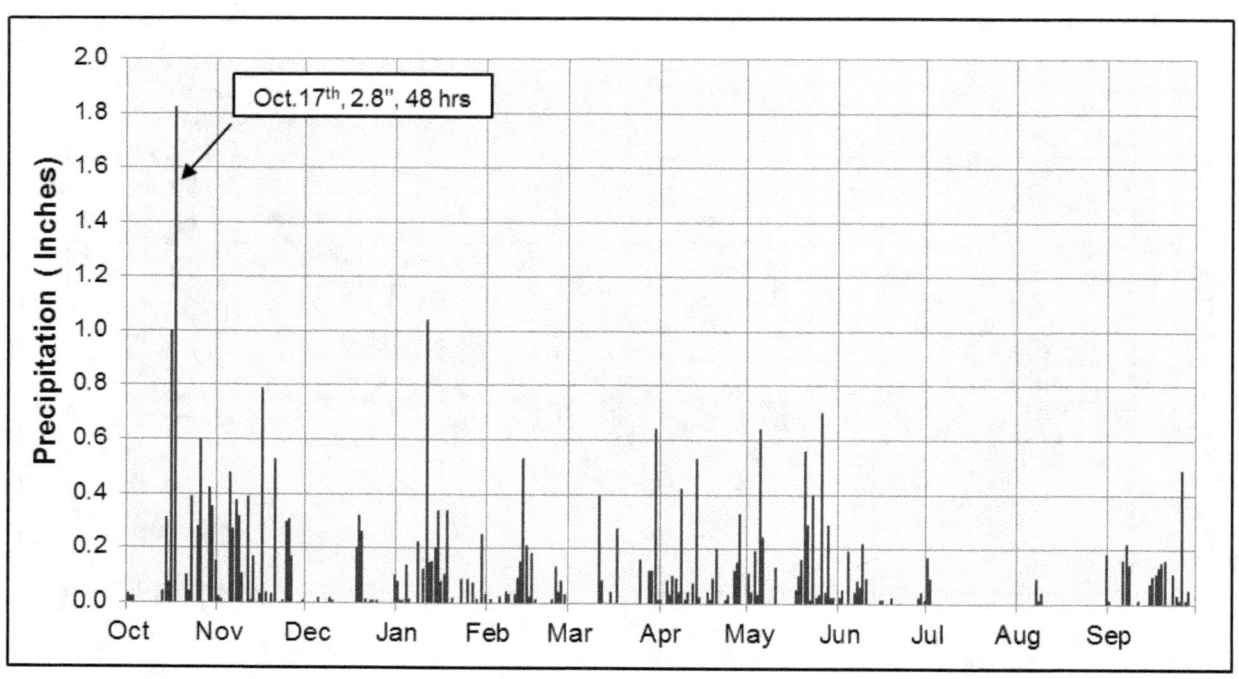

Figure B-4. Daily precipitation (inches) at Deer Park Ranger Station, Water Year 2010.

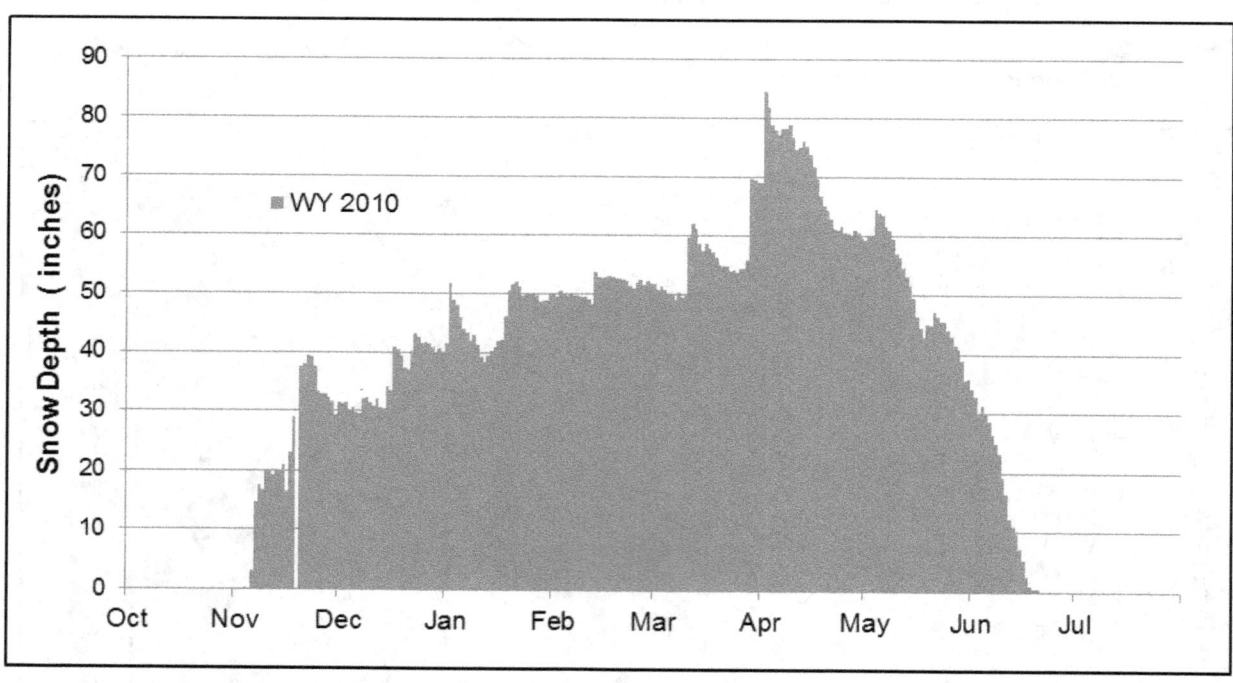

Figure B-5. Daily snow depth (inches) at Deer Park Ranger Station, Water Year 2010.

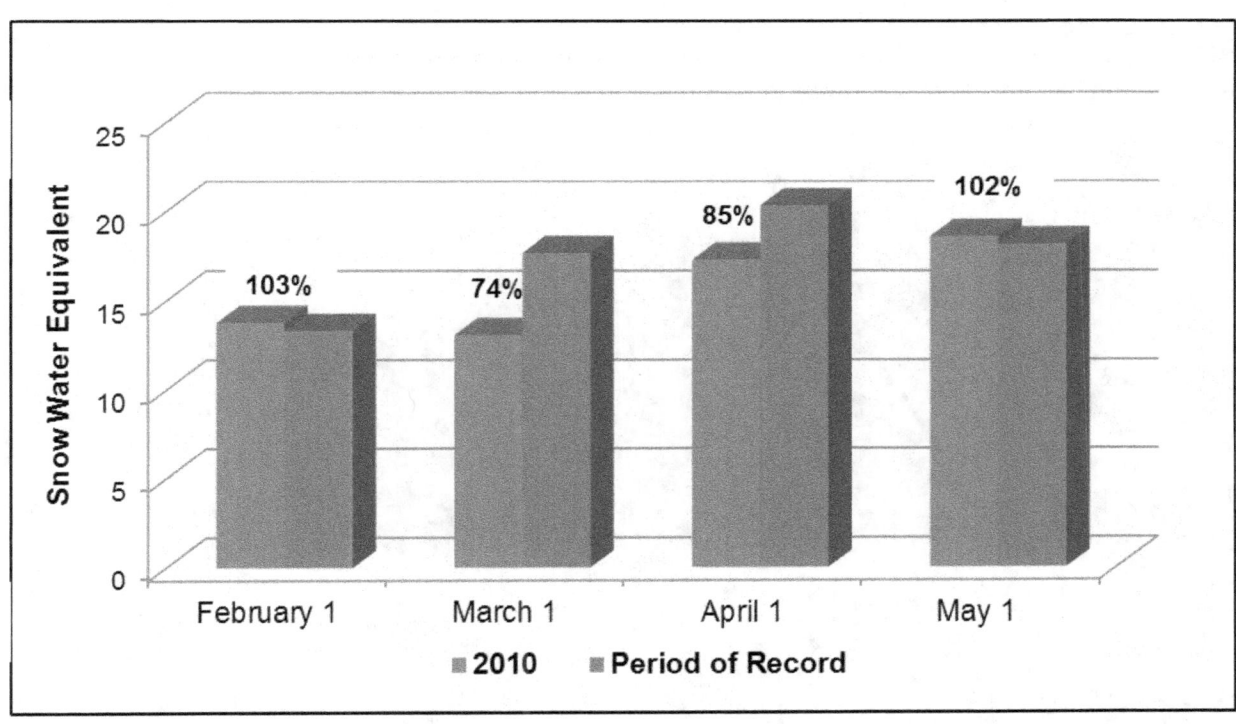

Figure B–6. First of the month snow water equivalent at Deer Park Snow Course in Water Year 2010, compared with the period of record (1949-2010).

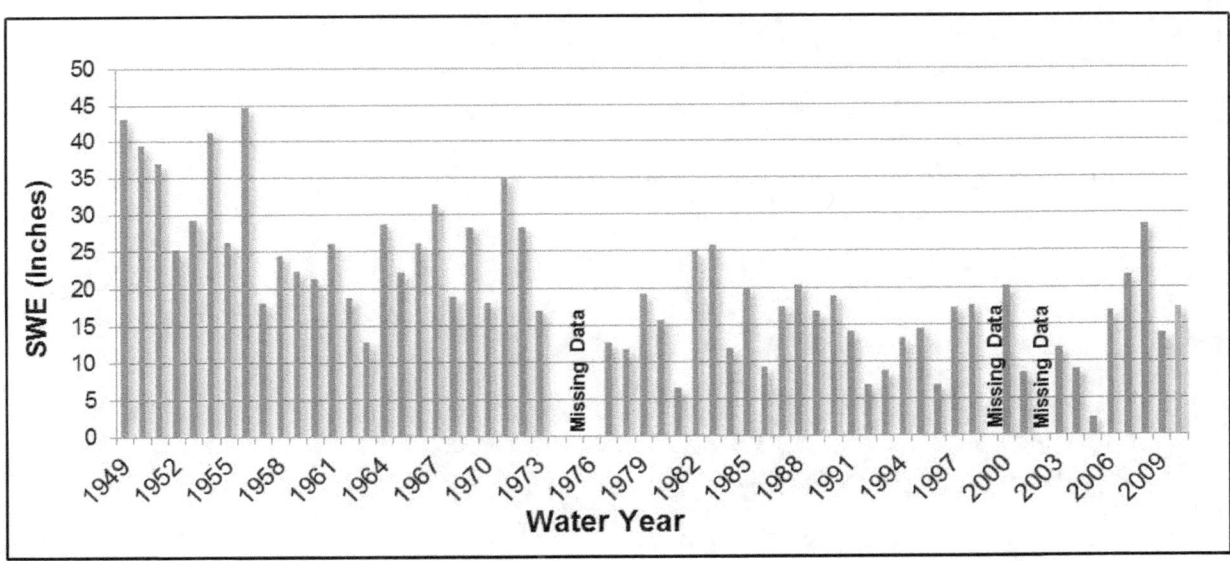

Figure B-7. April 1st snow water equivalent at the Deer Park Snow Course for the period of record (1949 - 2010). Highlighted column indicates Water 2010. No data were available for water years 1974-1976, 1999 and 2002.

Appendix C: Deer Park Road - Water Year 2010.

Temperatures ranged from an extreme low of 14.8°F during a particularly cold period in mid-December, to a high of 88.2°F in mid-August (Table C-1). Data from this station reflected the warmer than normal conditions in the months of January, February and March (4.2°, 4.0° and 2.6°F warmer than average), and the unusually cool late spring and early summer (April, -0.1°, May -1.5°, and June -3.0°F)(Figure C-1). Winter months were generally above freezing except for an extended period in early December (Figure C-2). The Deer Park Road, reflected similar late summer conditions as the Elwha Ranger Station, with warmer than average conditions in July and August (+ 2.4° and 1.7°) (Figure C-1). These were the only two sites in the park reflecting warmer than normal conditions during this period, revealing a different temperature regime occurring in the northeast portion of the Olympic Peninsula during this period.

The Deer Park Road, with 43.3 inches of total precipitation, was the driest station in the park during 2010 (Table 4 and Figure 14). The months of July and August were particularly dry (60% and 33% of average), and the relatively dry month of September received unusual amounts of rainfall (2.3 inches, 209% of average)(Figures C-3 and C-4). Both the Deer Park Road and Deer Park Ranger Stations sites recorded a high precipitation event on October 17, which was not noteworthy at other stations but was one of the highest rainfall events in these particular stations (Figures B-3 and C-5).

Table C-1. Monthly summary data, Deer Park Road, Water Year 2010.

Season	Month & Year	Mean Air Temp °F	Max Daily Air Temp °F	Min Daily Air Temp °F	Precipitation (inches)
Fall	October 2009	45.2	60.8	33.0	5.3
	November 2009	38.7	63.7	26.0	12.3
Winter	December 2009	33.2	55.2	14.8	3.3
	January 2010	39.8	52.5	30.1	7.9
	February 2010	39.3	51.2	30.5	1.7
Spring	March 2010	38.1	61.1	25.3	3.0
	April 2010	39.3	64.2	25.7	2.4
	May 2010	43.8	63.2	27.9	3.4
Summer	June 2010	47.9	67.0	35.9	1.1
	July 2010	60.8	86.4	41.0	0.3
	August 2010	60.1	88.2	42.8	0.3
Fall	September 2010	52.6	74.6	42.6	2.3
Water Year Total		**44.9**	**88.2**	**14.8**	**43.2**

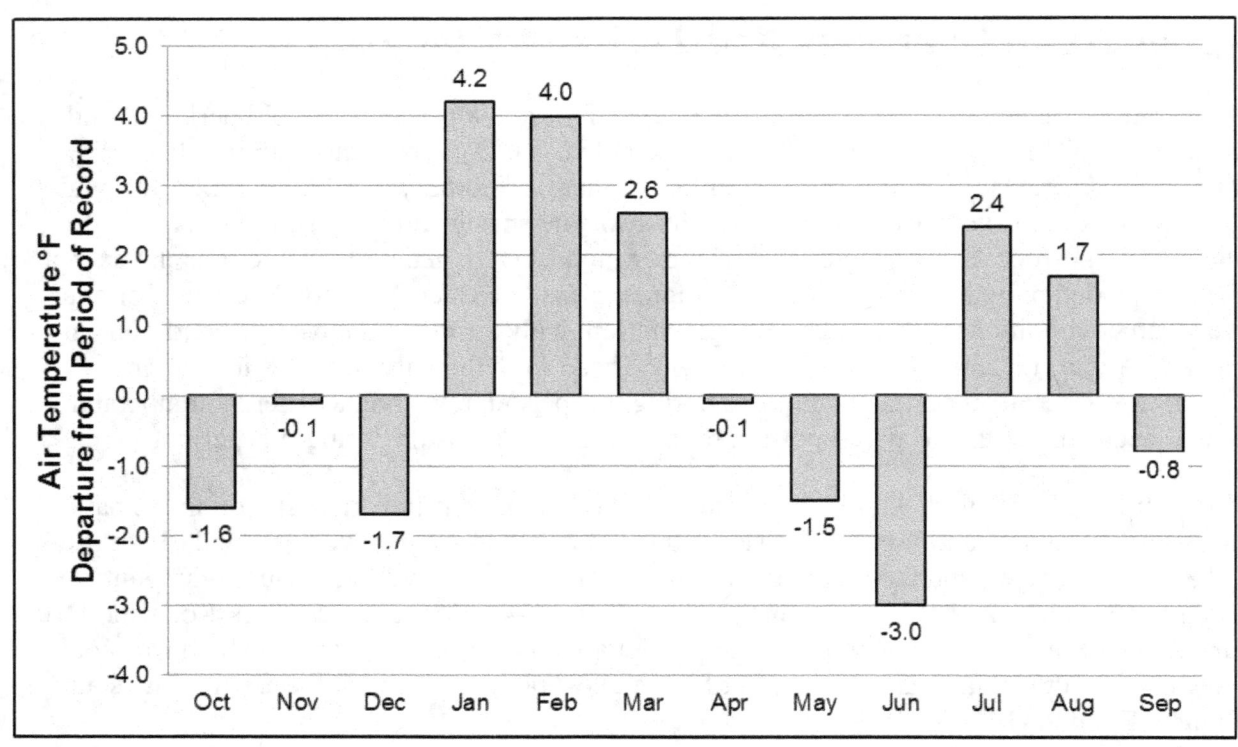

Figure C-1. Comparison of average monthly temperature (°F) for Deer Park Road in Water Year 2010 against monthly averages for the period of record (1999-2010).

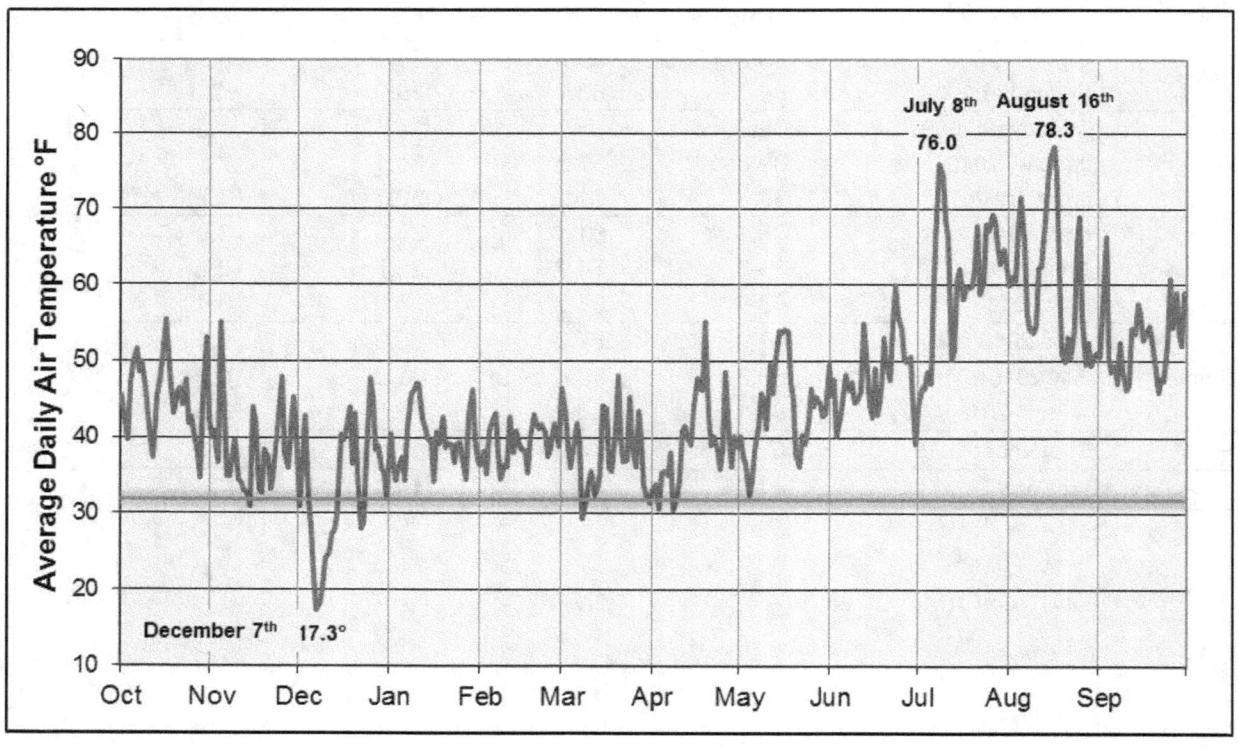

Figure C-2. Daily average air temp (°F) at Deer Park Road, Water Year 2010. Blue line indicates 32°F, the freezing point of water.

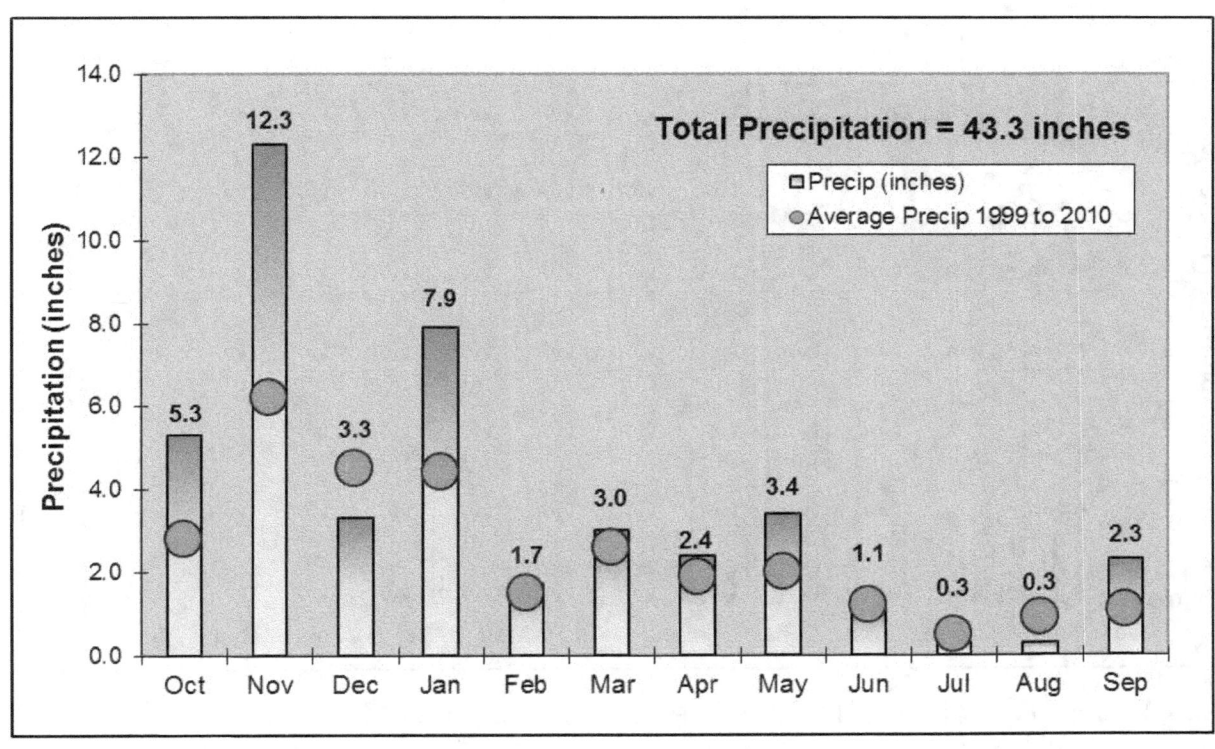

Figure C-3. Monthly precipitation values at Deer Park Road, Water Year 2010 compared to the monthly averages for the period of record (1999-2010).

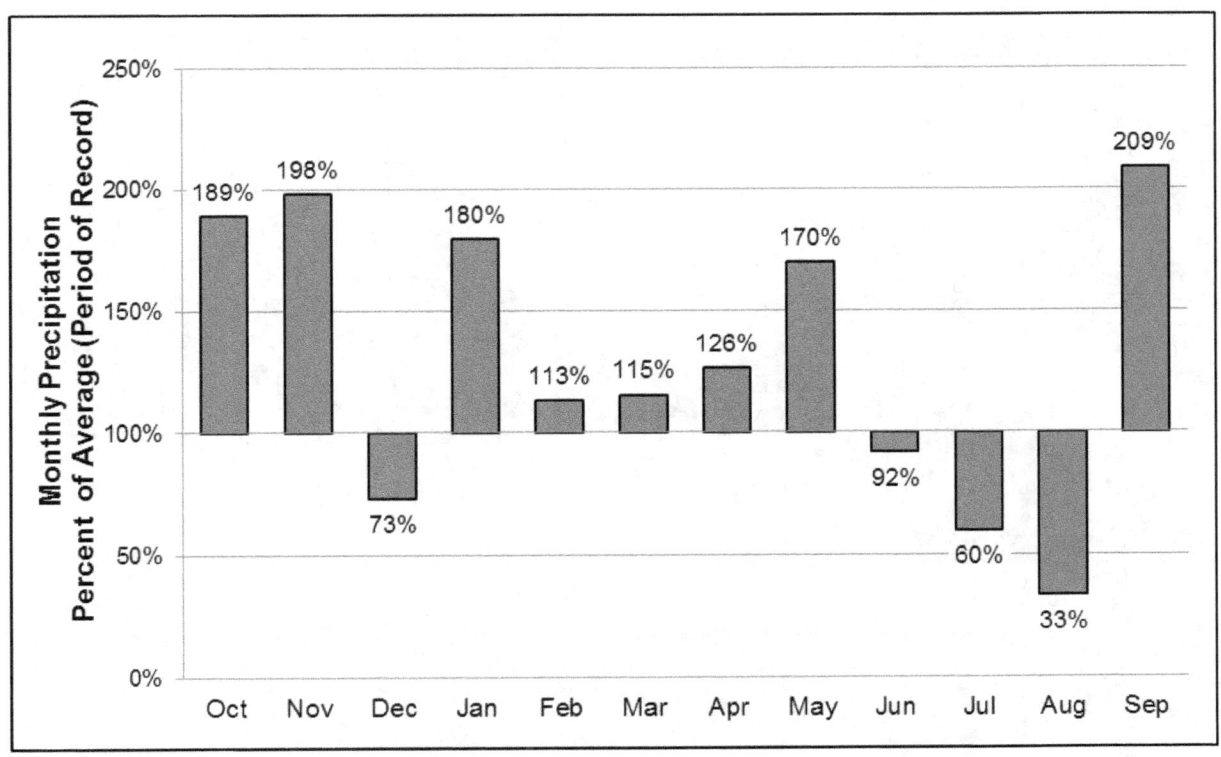

Figure C-4. Percent of average precipitation for the period of record (1999-2010) at Deer Park Road in Water Year 2010.

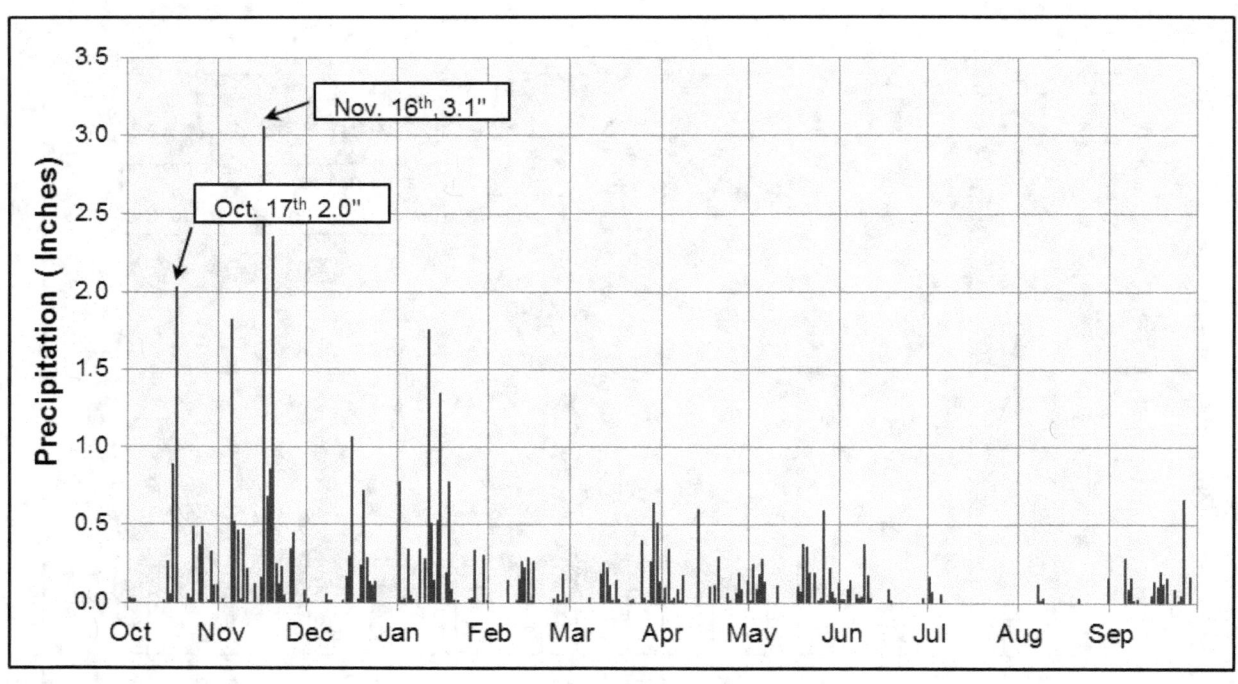

Figure C-5. Daily precipitation (inches) at Deer Park Road, Water Year 2010.

Appendix D: Hayes River Guard Station - Water Year 2010.

Temperatures ranged from an extreme low of 12.0°F during a particularly cold period in mid-December, to a high of 92.0° F on July 9 (Table D-1). Two prolonged periods of below freezing temperatures were recorded at Hayes Guard Station during the month of December (Figure D-1).

The station received 95.7 inches of total precipitation (Table D-1). The wettest month was November with 26.3 inches of precipitation (Figure D-2). The greatest period of rain occurred in the middle of November when two storms impacted the Olympic Peninsula over a 7 day period, dropping 14.1 inches of rain. The single heaviest day of rainfall was a storm on January 16, which dropped 3.9 inches of rain (Figure D-3).

Table D-1. Monthly summary data, Hayes River Guard Station, Water Year 2010.

Season	Month & Year	Mean Air Temp °F	Max Daily Air Temp °F	Min Daily Air Temp °F	Precipitation (inches)
Fall	October 2009	42.7	57.4	30.6	10.9
	November 2009	36.6	46.8	26.5	26.3
Winter	December 2009	29.1	39.9	12.0	6.6
	January 2010	37.8	45.9	30.6	17.1
	February 2010	37.0	45.2	26.9	6.5
Spring	March 2010	36.6	54.2	26.4	8.7
	April 2010	39.2	62.7	29.4	7.4
	May 2010	44.9	71.8	29.9	6.2
Summer	June 2010	52.2	77.5	35.9	1.1
	July 2010	59.9	92.0	40.2	0.2
	August 2010	58.6	90.3	38.0	0.5
Fall	September 2010	52.2	71.1	38.2	4.2
Water Year Total		**43.9**	**92.0**	**12.0**	**95.7**

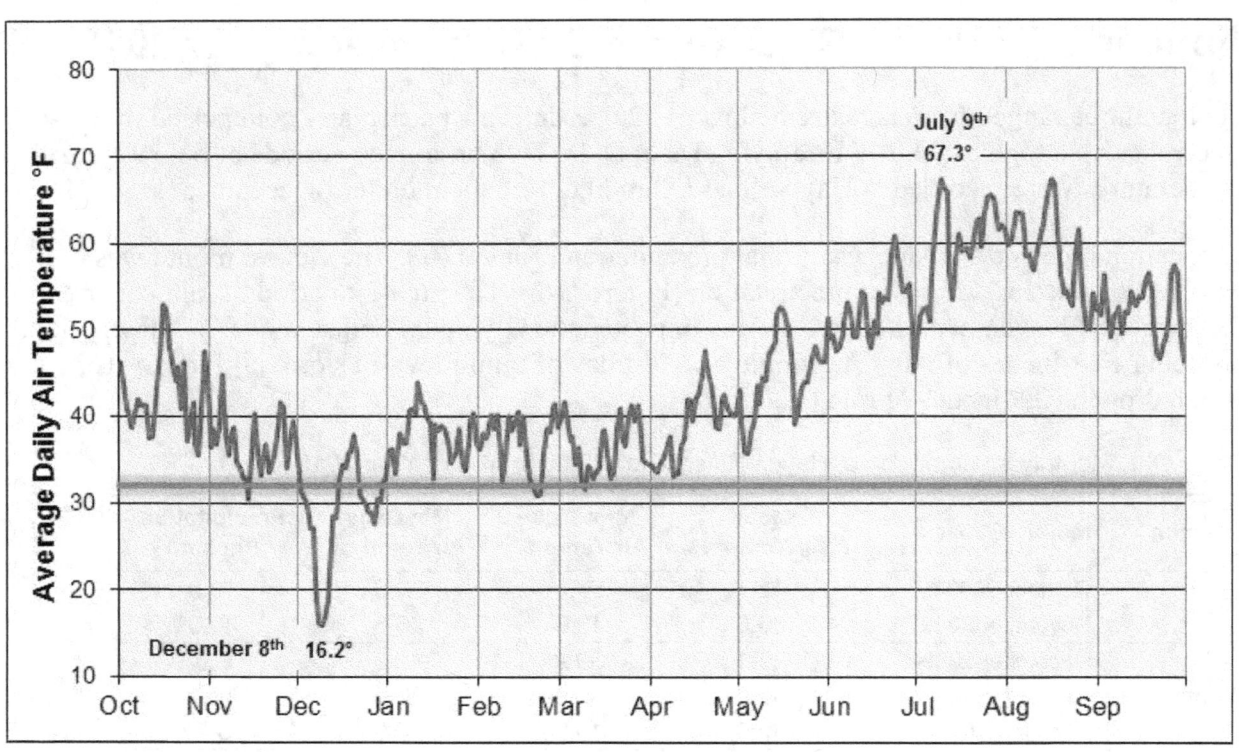

Figure D-1. Daily average air temp (°F) at Hayes River Guard Station, Water Year 2010. Blue line indicates 32°F, the freezing point of water.

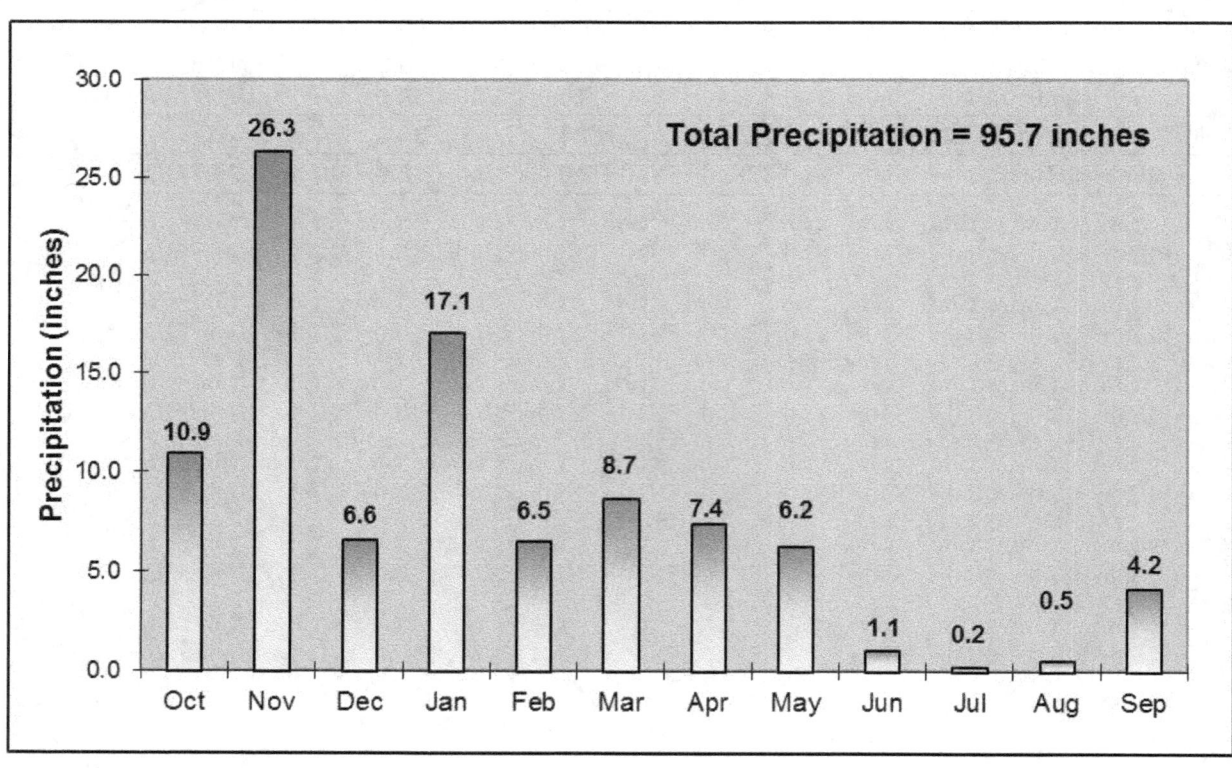

Figure D-2. Monthly precipitation values at Hayes River Guard Station, Water Year 2010.

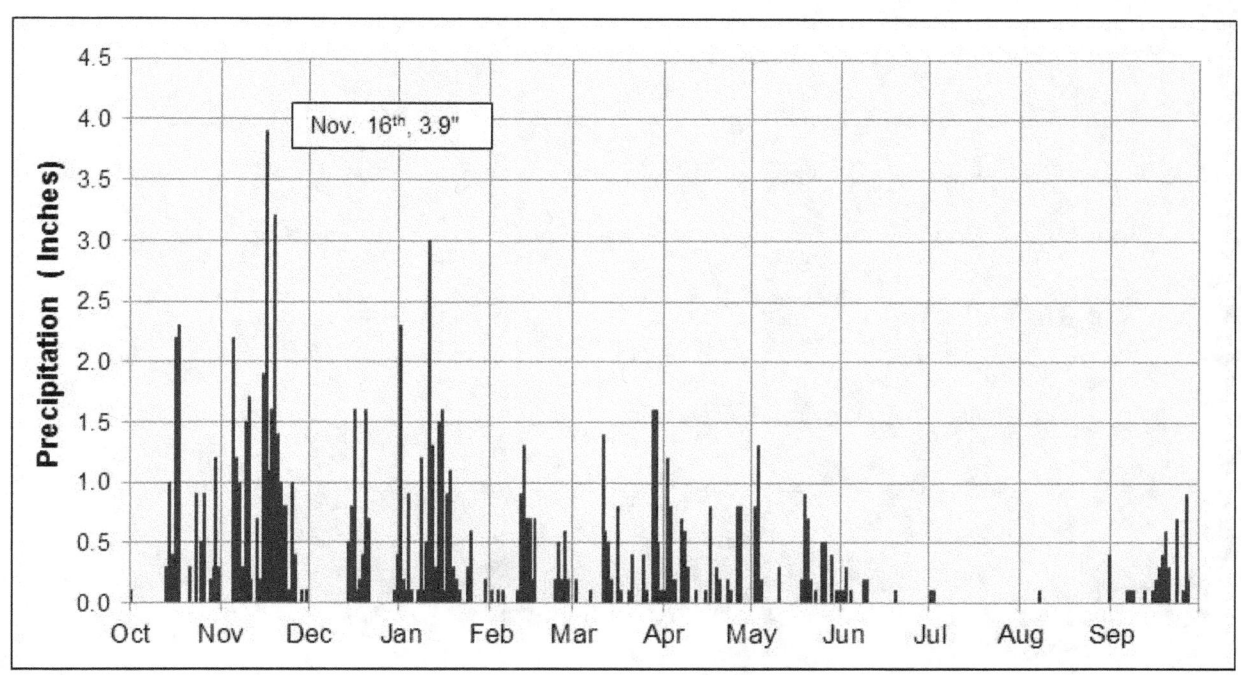

Figure D-3. Daily precipitation (inches) at Hayes River Guard Station, Water Year 2010.

Appendix E: Hoh Rainforest - Water Year 2010.

Temperatures ranged from an extreme low of 15.3°F in mid-December, to a high of 95.7°F on August 14 2010 (Table E-1). Data from this site reflected the warmer than average conditions in the months of January, February and March (4.4°, 2.4° and 0.8°F warmer than average), and the unusually cool spring and summer (Figure E-1). April through August had an average departure of -1.8°, with the coldest month in May with a departure of -2.9°F (Figure E-1). Air temperatures were generally above freezing with the exception of a prolonged period in early to mid-December (Figure E-2).

The Hoh Rainforest received 134.6 inches of rainfall in Water Year 2010 (Figure E-3). Late spring (April and May), were both unusually wet (180% of average), while summer months were generally drier than normal, especially in the month of July (Figure E-4). The first few days of that month received 0.25 inches of rain, followed by 32 days with little or no appreciable precipitation (Figure E-5). Dry conditions ended in September, when the Hoh received unusual amounts of rainfall (7.1 inches, 178% of average) (Figure E-4). The greatest period of rain occurred when two storms over seven days dropped 17.8 inches of rain between November 15 and 21, 2009. The single heaviest day of rainfall was on January 11, with 4.7 inches of rain (Figure E-5).

Table E-1. Monthly summary data, Hoh Rainforest, Water Year 2010.

Season	Month & Year	Mean Air Temp °F	Max Daily Air Temp °F	Min Daily Air Temp °F	Precipitation (inches)
Fall	October 2009	45.5	63.9	30.8	15.2
	November 2009	42.4	60.8	30.4	32.6
Winter	December 2009	34.1	50.5	15.3	8.5
	January 2010	43.7	54.5	30.4	21.3
	February 2010	42.3	59.4	28.3	9.4
Spring	March 2010	42.3	67.6	28.4	12.1
	April 2010	43.9	69.4	29.8	13.3
	May 2010	47.6	68.6	33.1	9.9
Summer	June 2010	53.2	75.8	37.2	2.6
	July 2010	58.3	91.9	40.5	0.3
	August 2010	58.0	95.7	37.1	2.3
Fall	September 2010	55.1	77.3	41.4	7.1
Water Year Total		**47.2**	**95.7**	**15.3**	**134.4**

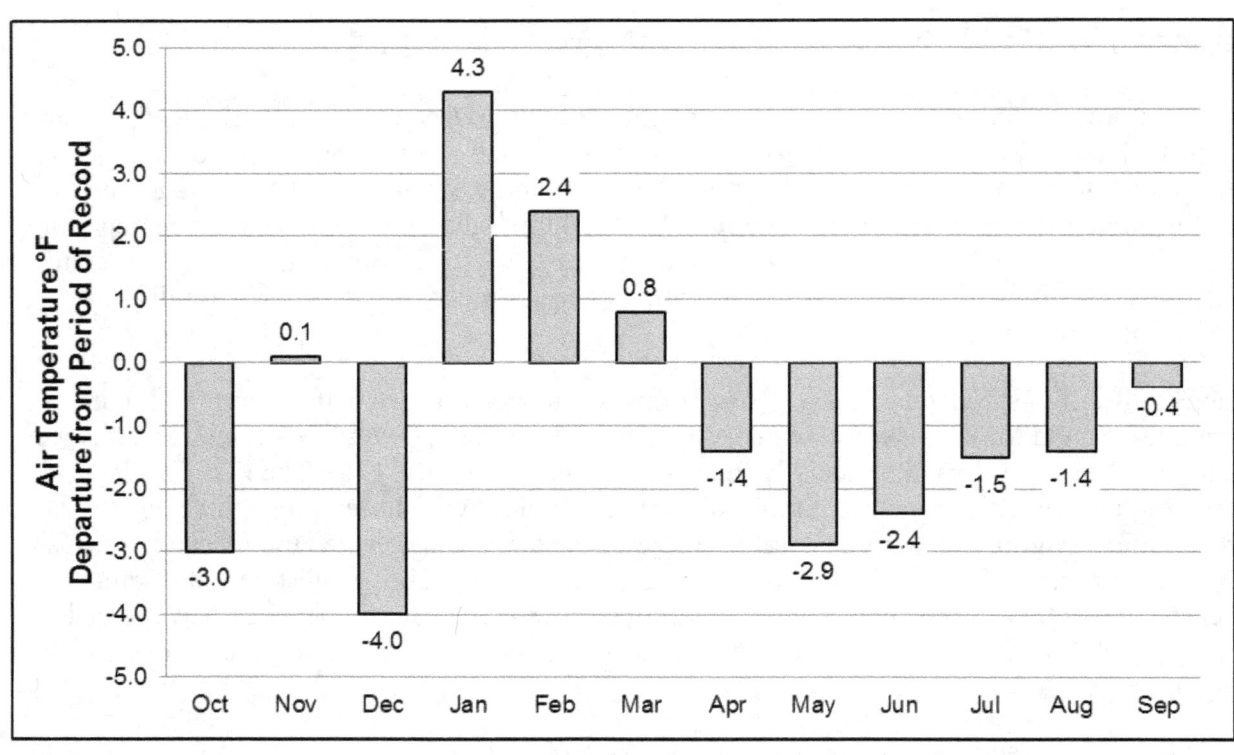

Figure E-1. Comparison of average monthly temperature (°F) for the Hoh Rainforest in Water Year 2010 against monthly averages for the period of record (1999-2010).

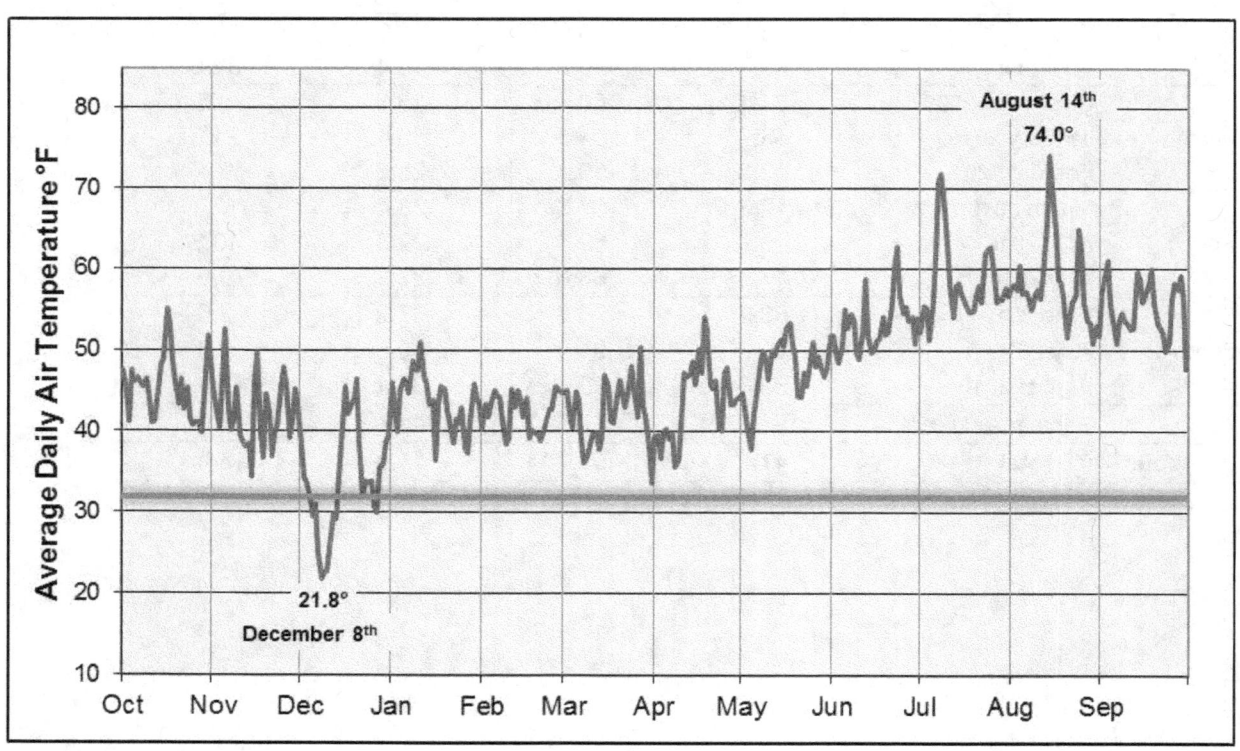

Figure E-2. Daily average air temp (°F) at the Hoh Rainforest, Water Year 2010. Blue line indicates 32°F, the freezing point of water.

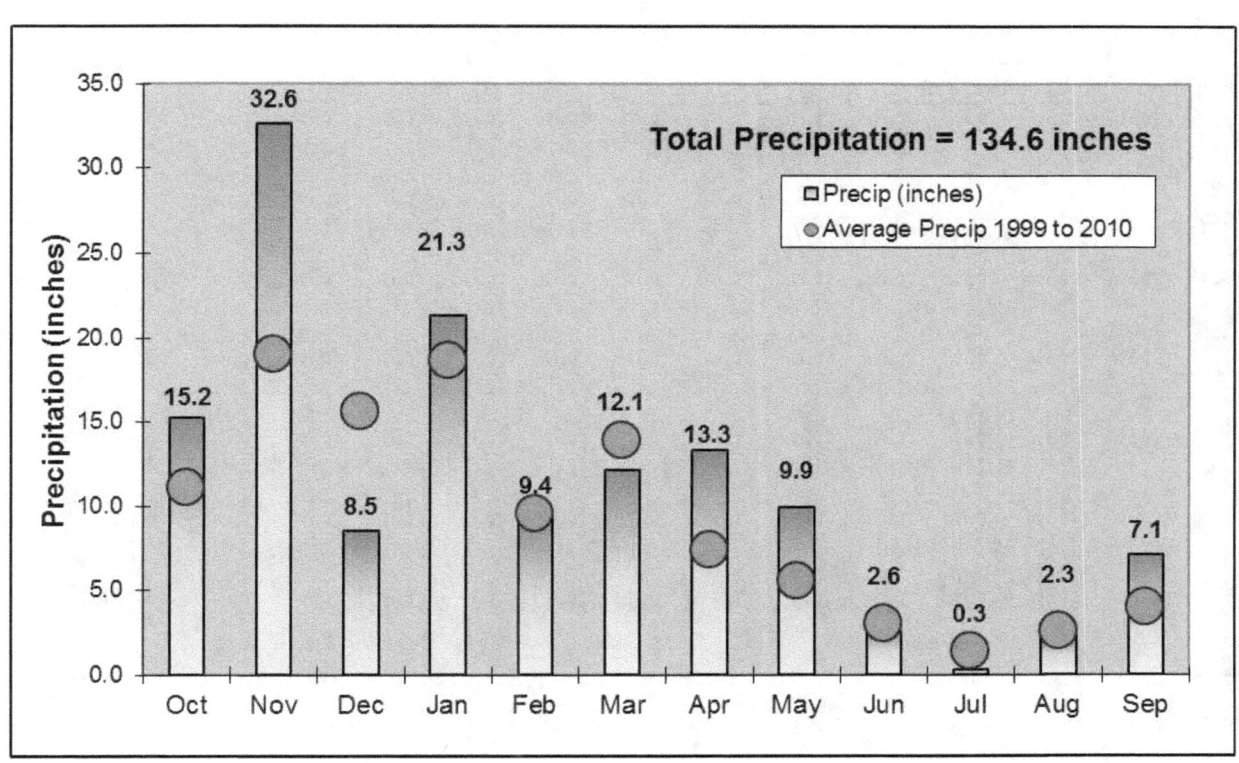

Figure E-3. Monthly precipitation values at the Hoh Rainforest, Water Year 2010 compared to the monthly averages for the period of record (1999-2010).

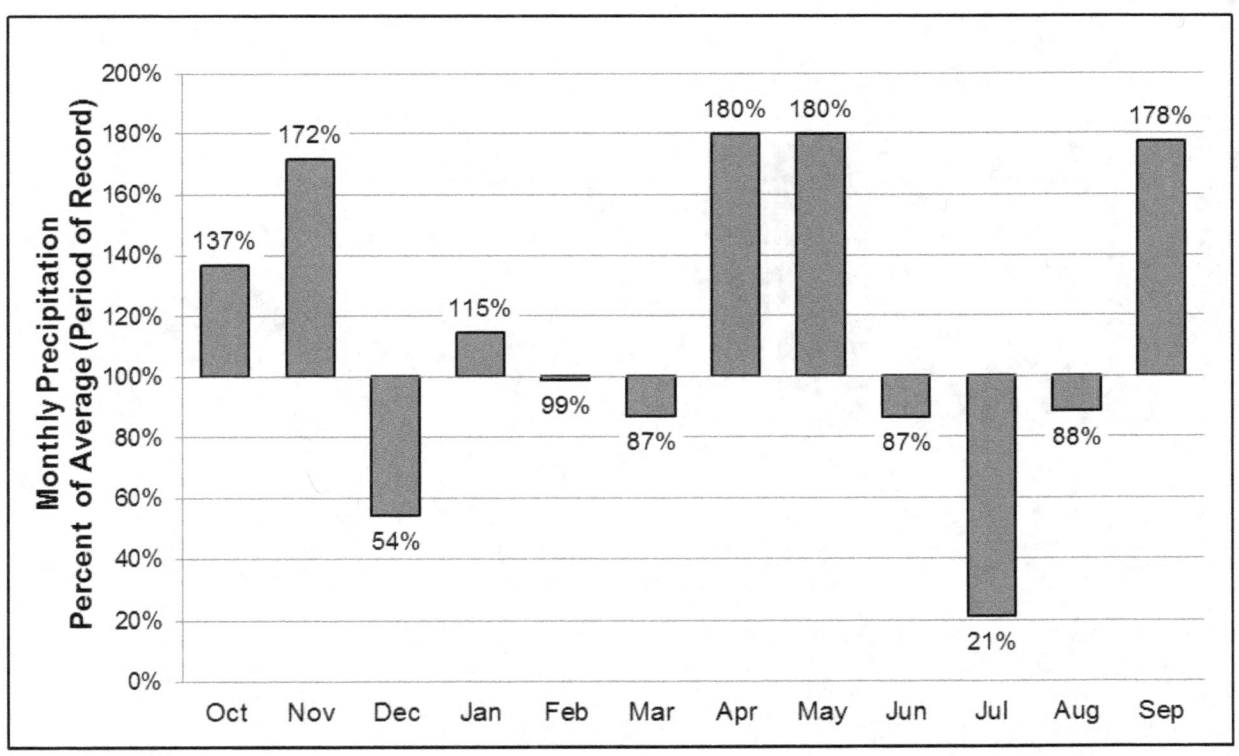

Figure E-4. Percent of average for the period of record (1999-2010) for precipitation at the Hoh Rainforest in Water Year 2010.

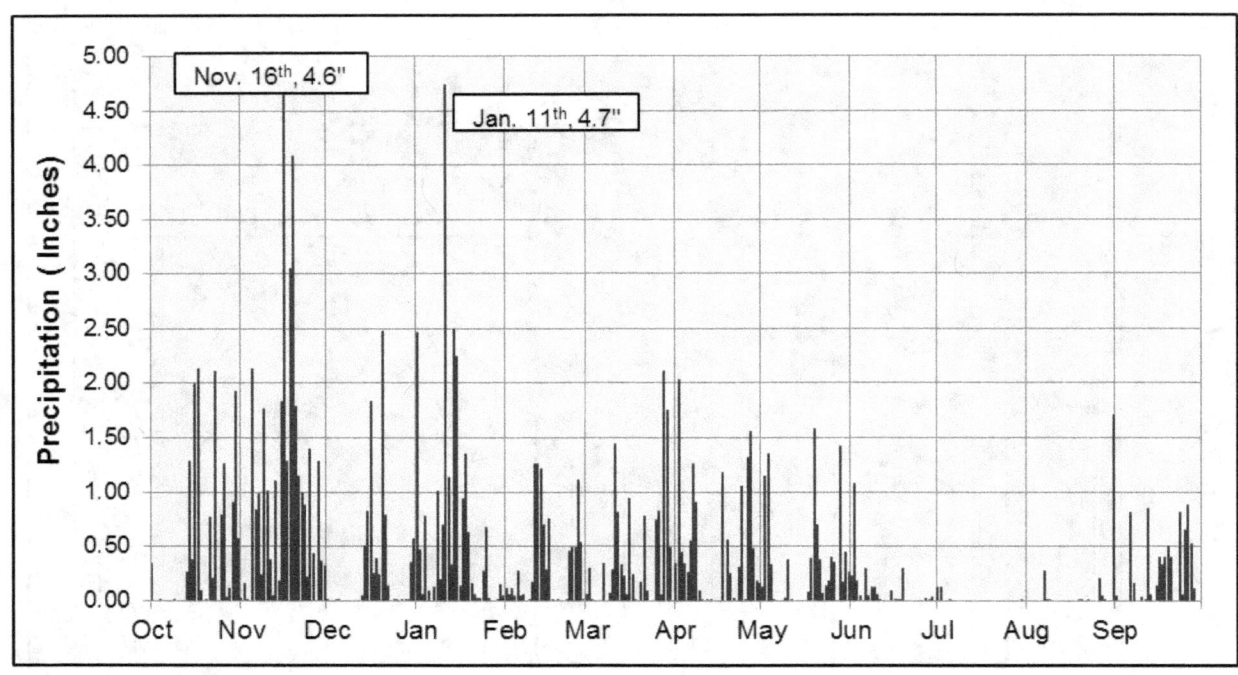

Figure E-5. Daily precipitation (inches) at the Hoh Rainforest, Water Year 2010.

Appendix F: Kalaloch Ranger Station - Water Year 2010.

Water Year 2010 was the second year of operation for this automated weather station. The current station replaces a manual station operated by Kalaloch rangers since 1966.

The low temperature recorded at Kalaloch Ranger Station in 2010 was 20.7°F on December 7, 2009 (Table F-1). This was an unusually low temperature for a coastal site adjacent to the Pacific Ocean and daily average air temperature remained below freezing for a seven day period (Figure F-1). A maximum summer temperature was not recorded this year, due to the failure of the temperature sensor. The failure possibly relates to high humidity conditions during spring and summer months. These conditions have plagued the Vaisala HMP 45C temperature and relative humidity probes installed at many NPS sites at Olympic.

The Kalaloch area received 107.8 inches of rainfall in Water Year 2010 (Figure F-2). Late spring and early summer were both unusually wet, with the combined months of April, May & June 132% of average (Figure F-3). Late summer was generally drier than normal. The relatively dry month of September received unusual amounts of rainfall (7.3 inches, 165% of average)(figure F-3). The greatest period of rain occurred when two storms over 5 days dropped 13.8 inches of rain between November 15 and November 21, 2009. The single heaviest day of rainfall was a storm on January 11th, which dropped 4.3 inches of rain (Figure F-4).

Table F-1. Monthly summary data, Kalaloch Ranger Station, Water Year 2010.

Season	Month & Year	Mean Air Temp °F	Max Daily Air Temp °F	Min Daily Air Temp °F	Precipitation (inches)
Fall	October 2009	50.1	64.2	36.3	12.4
	November 2009	45.9	65.1	33.8	24.8
Winter	December 2009	37.6	52.7	20.7	5.5
	January 2010	47.3	56.8	34.3	15.9
	February 2010	45.4	57.6	30.2	7.7
Spring	March 2010	45.0	62.2	31.3	9.2
	April 2010	46.4	61.0	32.5	9.5
	May 2010	48.7	58.9	33.2	8.2
Summer	June 2010	49.9	59.2	41.7	4.2
	July 2010				0.4
	August 2010				2.6
Fall	September 2010				7.3
Water Year Total		**46.3**	**65.1**	**20.7**	**107.8**

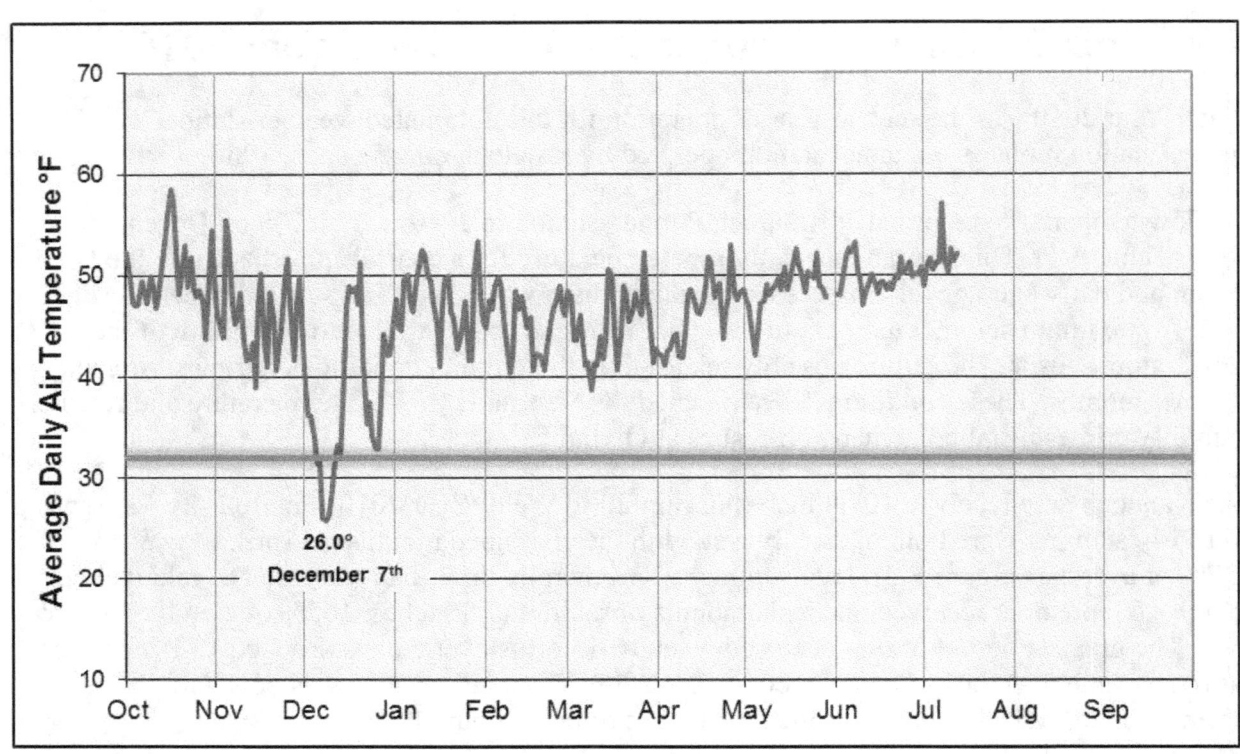

Figure F-1. Daily average air temp (°F) at the Kalaloch Ranger Station, Water Year 2010. Blue line indicates 32°F, the freezing point of water.

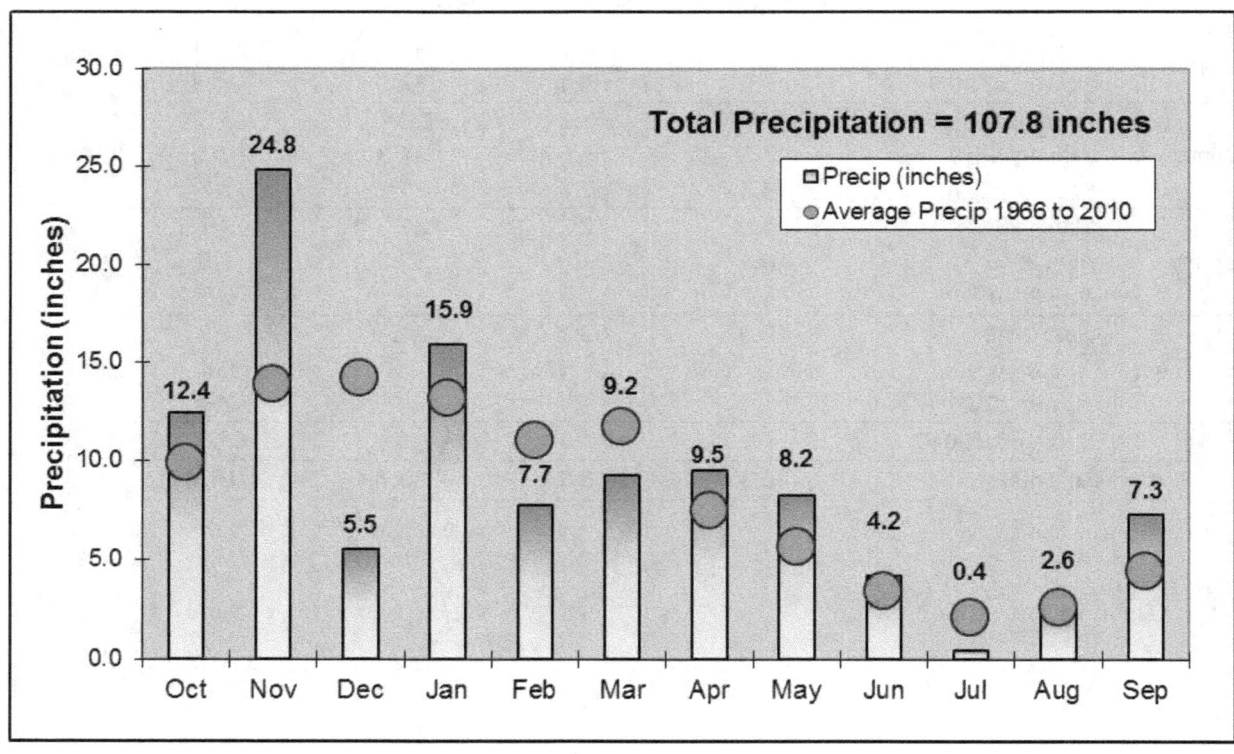

Figure F-2. Monthly precipitation values at the Kalaloch Ranger Station, Water Year 2010 compared to the monthly averages for the period of record (1966-2010).

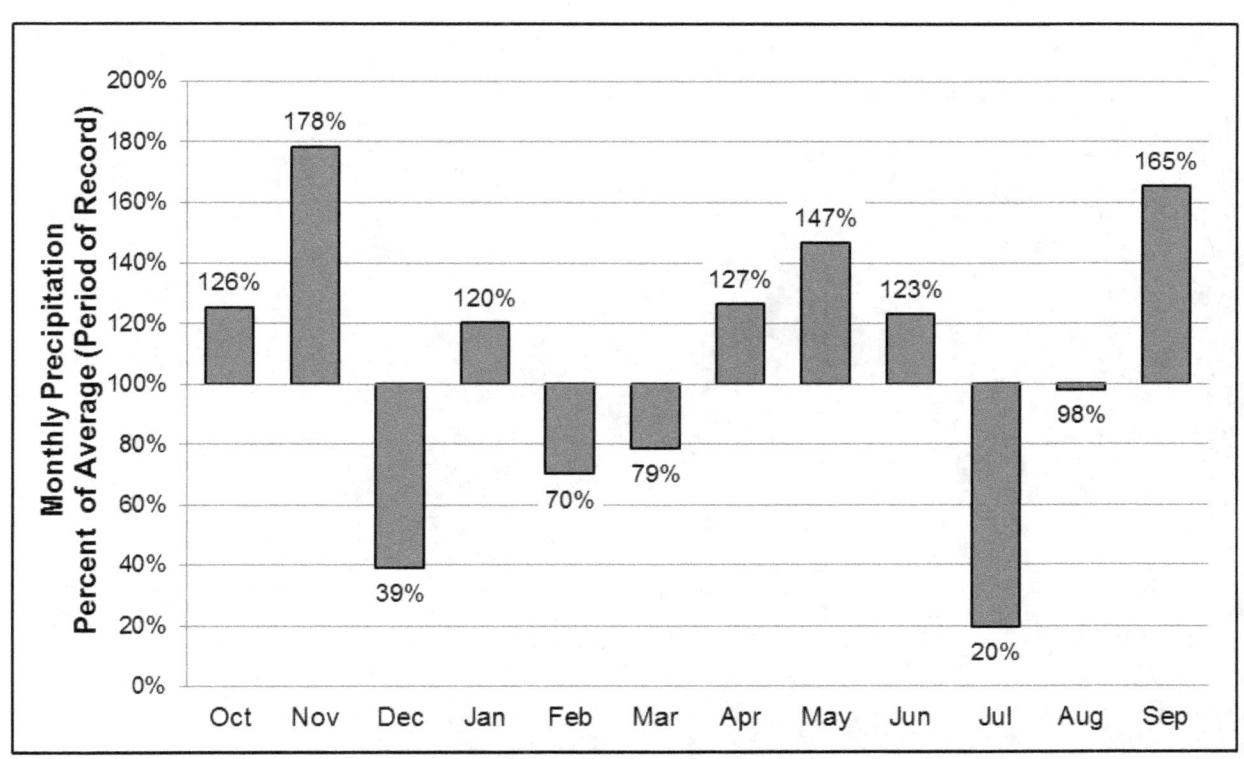

Figure F-3. Percent departure from the period of record (1966-2010) for precipitation at the Kalaloch Ranger Station in Water Year 2010.

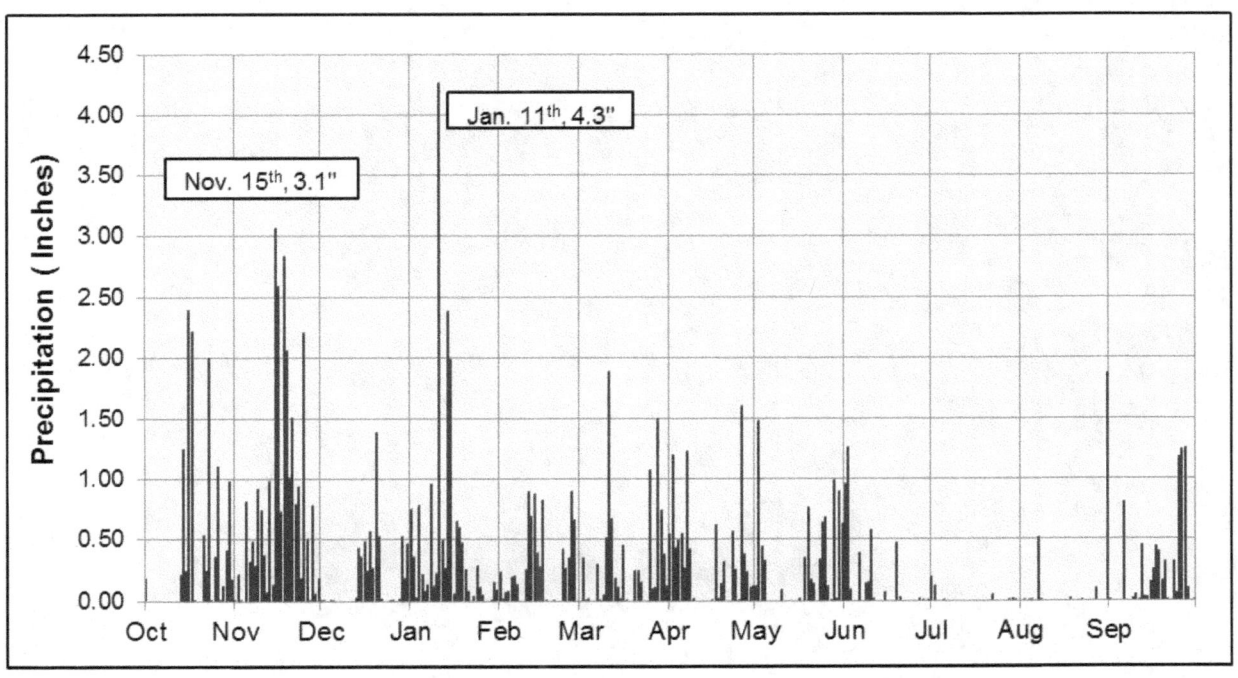

Figure F-4. Daily precipitation (inches) at the Kalaloch Ranger Station, Water Year 2011.

Appendix G: Ozette Ranger Station - Water Year 2010.

Temperatures ranged from a low of 21.8° F in mid-December, to a high of 93.6° F in mid-August (Table G-1). December at Ozette was particularly cold, with a temperature departure of 6.4°F below the 8 year record (Figure G-1). Several days in early December were the only period where average daily temperatures remained below freezing (Figure G-2). January and February were warmer than average (3.9°, 1.3°F) however the spring and summer months remained well below average (March, April, May -1.8°, June, July, August -2.4°F)(Figure G-1).

It was generally a wet year at Ozette, with eight of the twelve months receiving above average precipitation (Figures G-3 and G-4). The exceptions were December (68% of average) and July (20% of average) (Figure G-4). The greatest departure was November, with 24.4 inches of rainfall (180% of the average rainfall measured at this site since 1982). The other notable month was September 2010, with 6.7 inches of rain (Table G-1). This normally dry month received 233% of its average precipitation. The greatest period of precipitation occurred between November 15th and 21st, when two storms dropped 12.3 inches of rain. The single heaviest day of rainfall was on November 18th with 3.5 inches of precipitation (Figure G-5).

On December 10, 2009 a new temperature and relative humidity sensor was installed at this station. A Vaisala HMP 35C was replaced with a model 45C to increase reliability of humidity measurements between 94% and 100%. In addition, a backup temperature sensor (Campbell Scientific 107B thermistor temperature probe) was installed. Data logger memory problems led to a small loss of data in December, May and June.

Table G-1. Monthly summary data, Ozette Ranger Station, Water Year 2010.

Season	Month & Year	Mean Air Temp °F	Max Daily Air Temp °F	Min Daily Air Temp °F	Precipitation (inches)
Fall	October 2009	50.1	67.0	34.6	12.0
	November 2009	46.9	59.7	33.3	24.4
Winter	December 2009	----[a]	----[a]	21.8[a]	7.5[d]
	January 2010	45.8	53.6	31.4	16.5
	February 2010	45.2	59.6	27.6	6.8
Spring	March 2010	44.6	63.6	29.1	8.9
	April 2010	46.7	65.0	29.5	8.6
	May 2010	----[b]	----[b]	----[b]	7.6[d]
Summer	June 2010	----[c]	----[c]	----[c]	4.3[d]
	July 2010	56.3	90.8	41.9	0.5
	August 2010	56.7	93.6	40.5	3.2
Fall	September 2010	56.7	75.0	40.7	6.7
Water Year Total		**49.0**	**93.6**	**21.8**	**96.2**

[a] 8 missing days of data in December

[b] 19 missing days of data in May

[c] 15 missing days of data in June

[d] Missing data were replaced with precipitation values from the nearby Quillayute Field COOP.

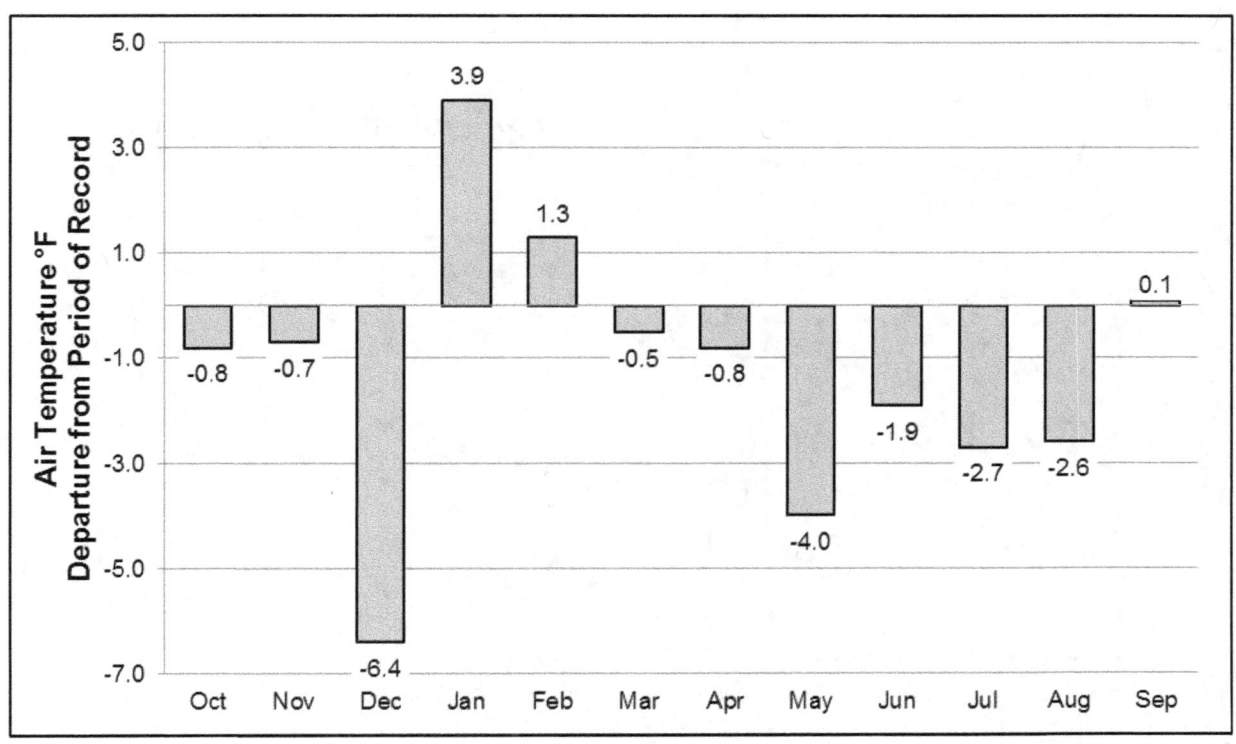

Figure G-1. Comparison of average monthly temperature (°F) for the Ozette Ranger Station in Water Year 2010 against monthly averages for the period of record (2004-2010).

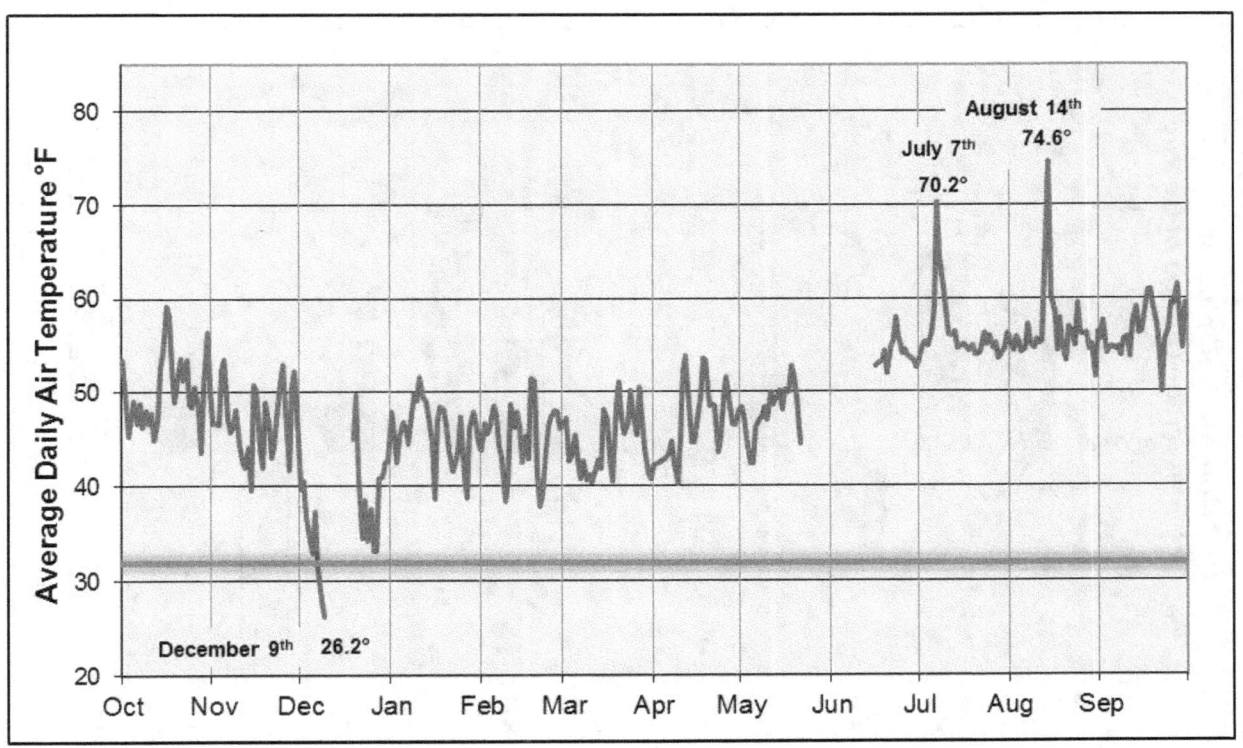

Figure G-2. Daily average air temp (°F) at the Ozette Ranger Station, Water Year 2010. Blue line indicates 32°F, the freezing point of water.

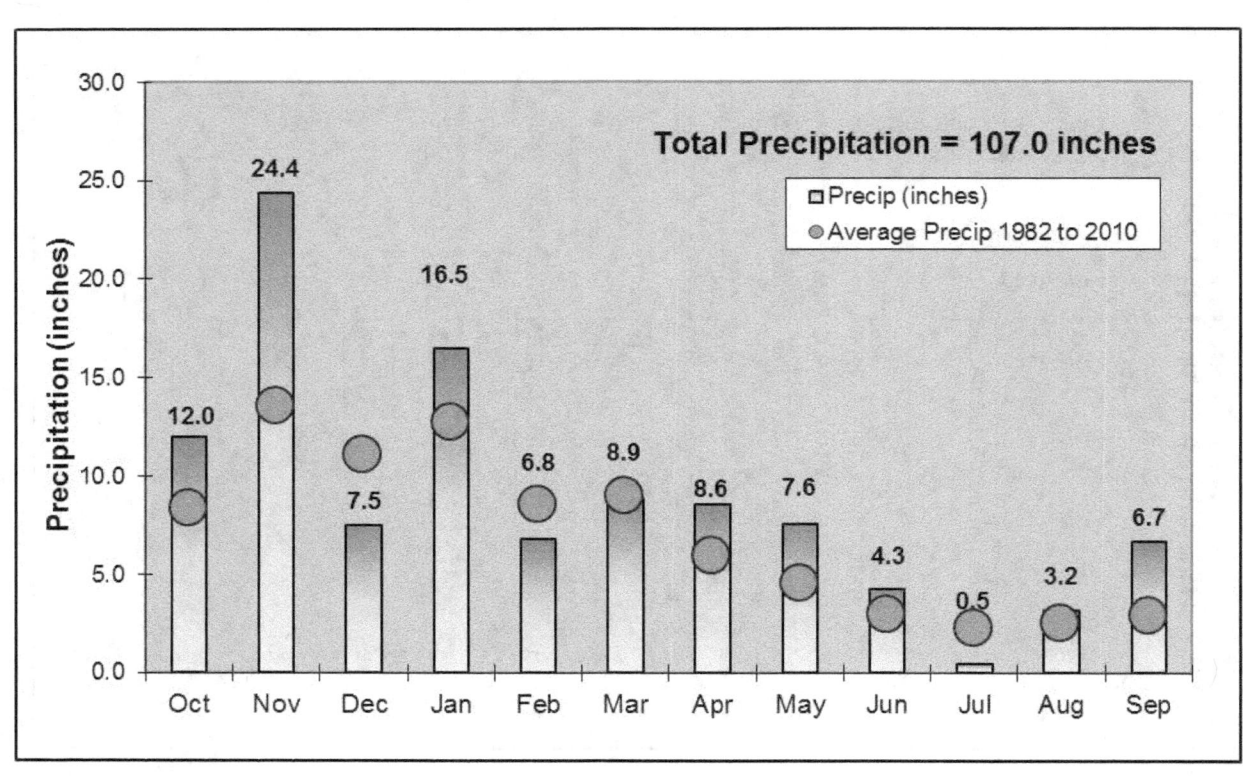

Figure G-3. Monthly precipitation values at the Ozette Ranger Station, Water Year 2010 compared to the monthly averages for the period of record (1982-2010).

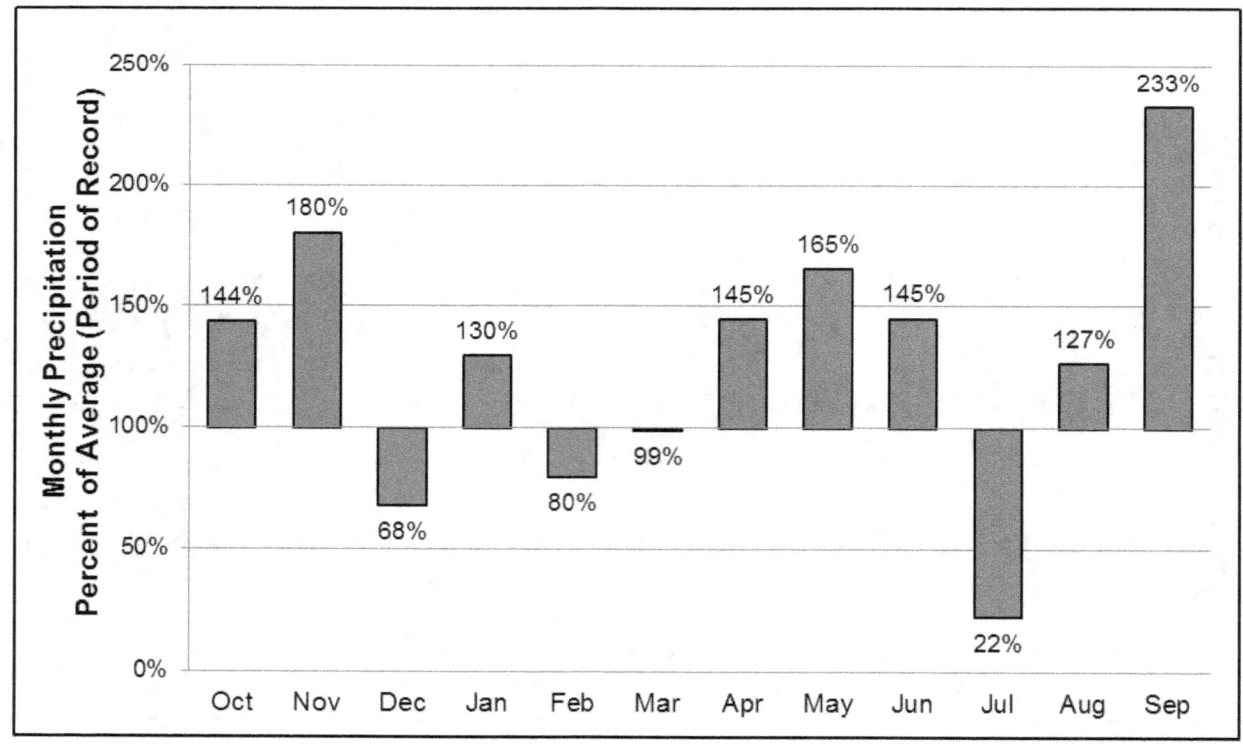

Figure G-4. Percent departure from the period of record (1982-2010) for precipitation at the Ozette Ranger Station in Water Year 2010.

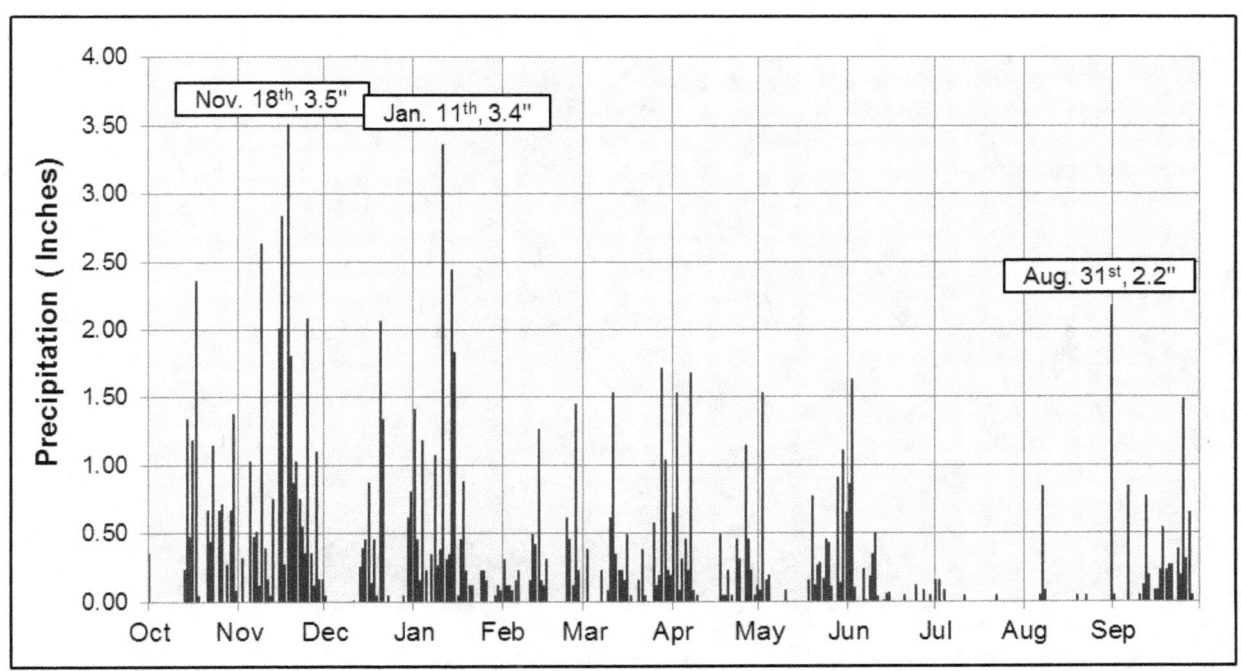

Figure G-5. Daily precipitation (inches) at the Ozette Ranger Station, Water Year 2010.

Appendix H: Quinault Rainforest - Water Year 2010.

Temperatures ranged from an extreme low of 16.6°F in mid-December, to a high of 97.5°F on August 14 (Table H-1). The station recorded a twelve day period of below freezing temperatures during the first half of December (Figure H-2). Data from this site reflected the warmer than average conditions in the months of January, February and March (8.4°, 4.4° and 2.0°F warmer than average), and the unusually cool spring and summer. April through August had an average departure of -1.2°F. The coldest month during this departure was May, at 2.4°F below average (Figure H-1).

The Quinault Rainforest received 137.2 inches of rainfall in Water Year 2010 (Figure H-3). Late spring (April and May), were both unusually wet (197% and 166% of average), while summer months were generally drier than normal, especially in the month of July (Figure H-4). The first 2 days of that month received 0.4 inches of rain, followed by 32 days with no appreciable precipitation (Figure H-5). Dry conditions ended in September, when the Quinault received unusual amounts of rain (7.4 inches, 218% of average) (Figure H-3). The greatest period of rain occurred when two storms over a seven day period dropped 16.9 inches of rain. The single heaviest day of rainfall was during this period, depositing 4.6 inches of rain on November 16 (Figure H-5).

In mid-October 2009, a mechanical failure of the tipping bucket switch occurred at the primary weather station at Bunch Field in the Quinault. The tipping bucket was not repaired until early July. Missing data were replaced using values from a research weather station near Irely Lake, 2.75 miles northeast (up valley) of the Bunch Field weather station.

Table H-1. Monthly summary data, Quinault Rainforest, Water Year 2010.

Season	Month & Year	Mean Air Temp °F	Max Daily Air Temp °F	Min Daily Air Temp °F	Precipitation (inches)
Fall	October 2009	49.2	71.0	36.0	18.4[a]
	November 2009	41.0	60.5	30.1	33.6[a]
Winter	December 2009	33.8	50.1	16.6	8.9[a]
	January 2010	45.4	54.3	32.9	21.9[a]
	February 2010	43.2	58.1	30.3	11.8[a]
Spring	March 2010	43.2	68.0	27.8	10.5[a]
	April 2010	45.1	70.1	31.6	12.8[a]
	May 2010	49.5	72.1	32.3	7.8[a]
Summer	June 2010	55.6	81.7	40.6	2.5[a]
	July 2010	60.5	95.6	44.5	0.4[a]
	August 2010	60.8	97.5	44.9	1.2
Fall	September 2010	58.2	80.0	44.9	7.4
Water Year Total		**48.8**	**97.5**	**16.6**	**137.2[a]**

[a] Precipitation data were interpolated from the Irely Lake Weather Station, located 2.75 miles northeast (up valley) of the Quinault Rainforest weather station at Bunch Field.

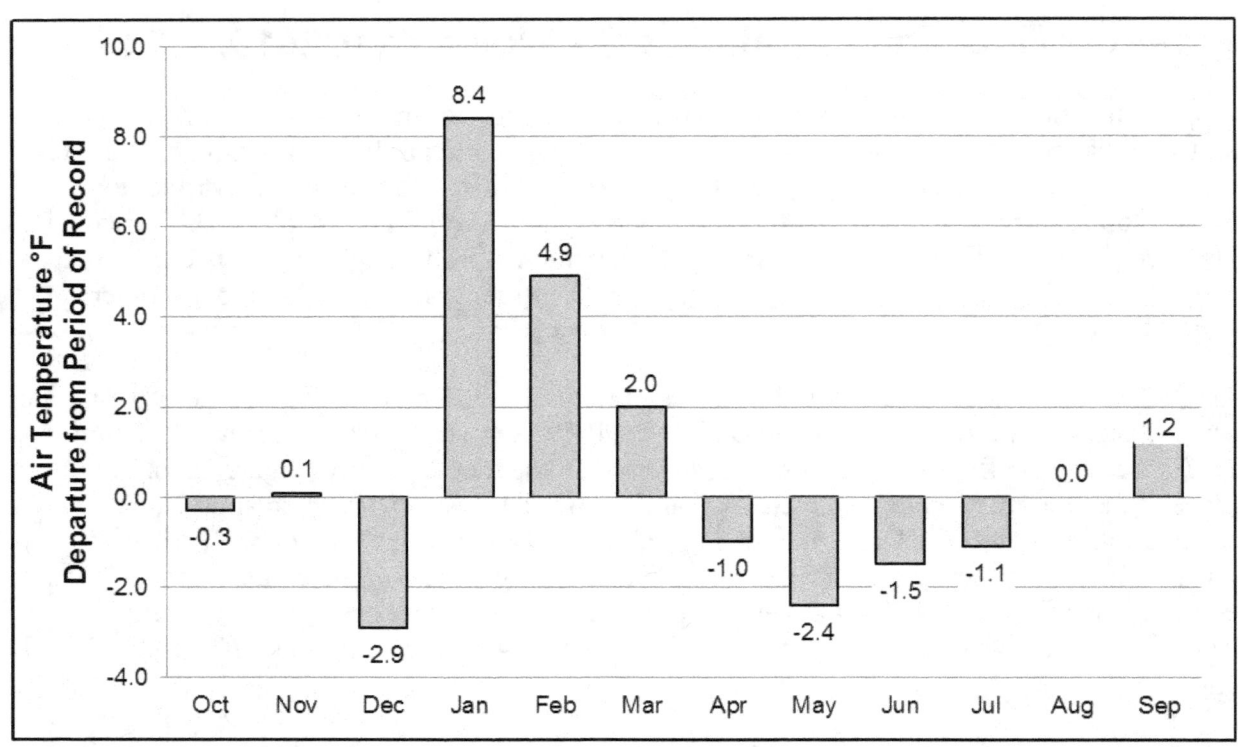

Figure H-1. Comparison of average monthly temperature (°F) for the Quinault Rainforest in Water Year 2010 against monthly averages for the period of record (1999-2010).

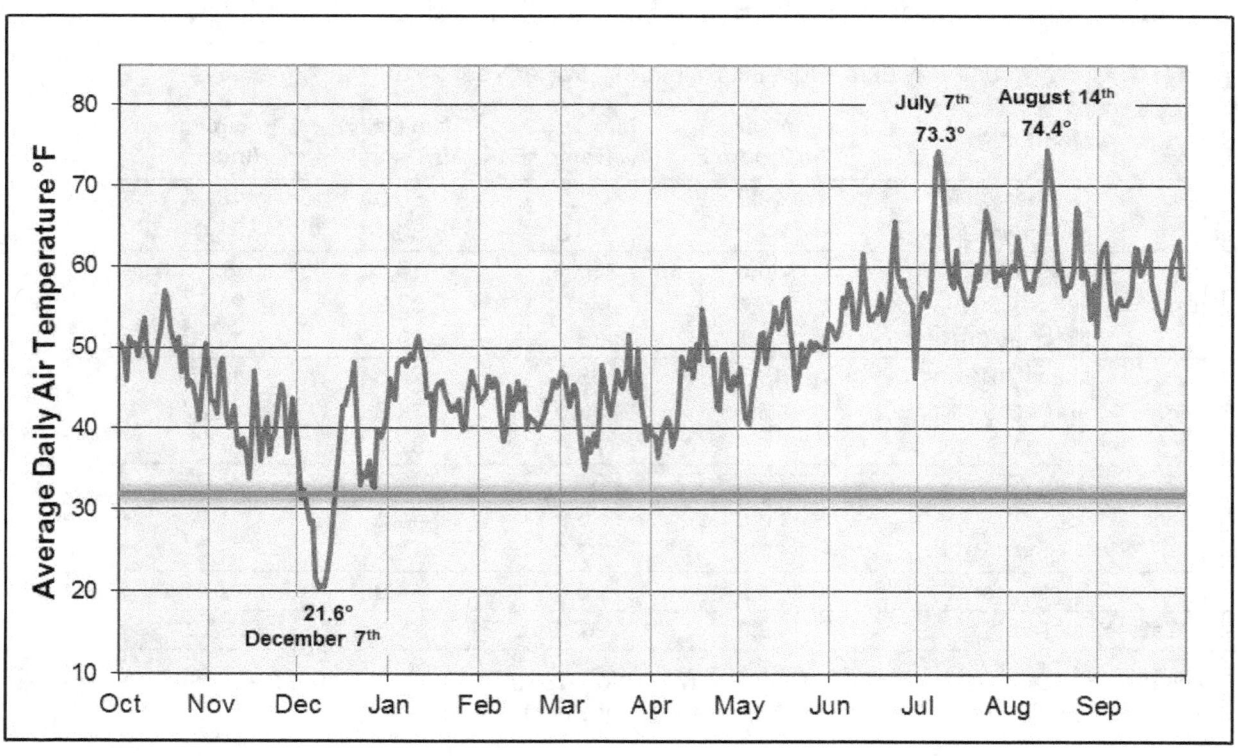

Figure H-2. Daily average air temp (°F) at the Quinault Rainforest, Water Year 2010. Blue line indicates 32°F, the freezing point of water.

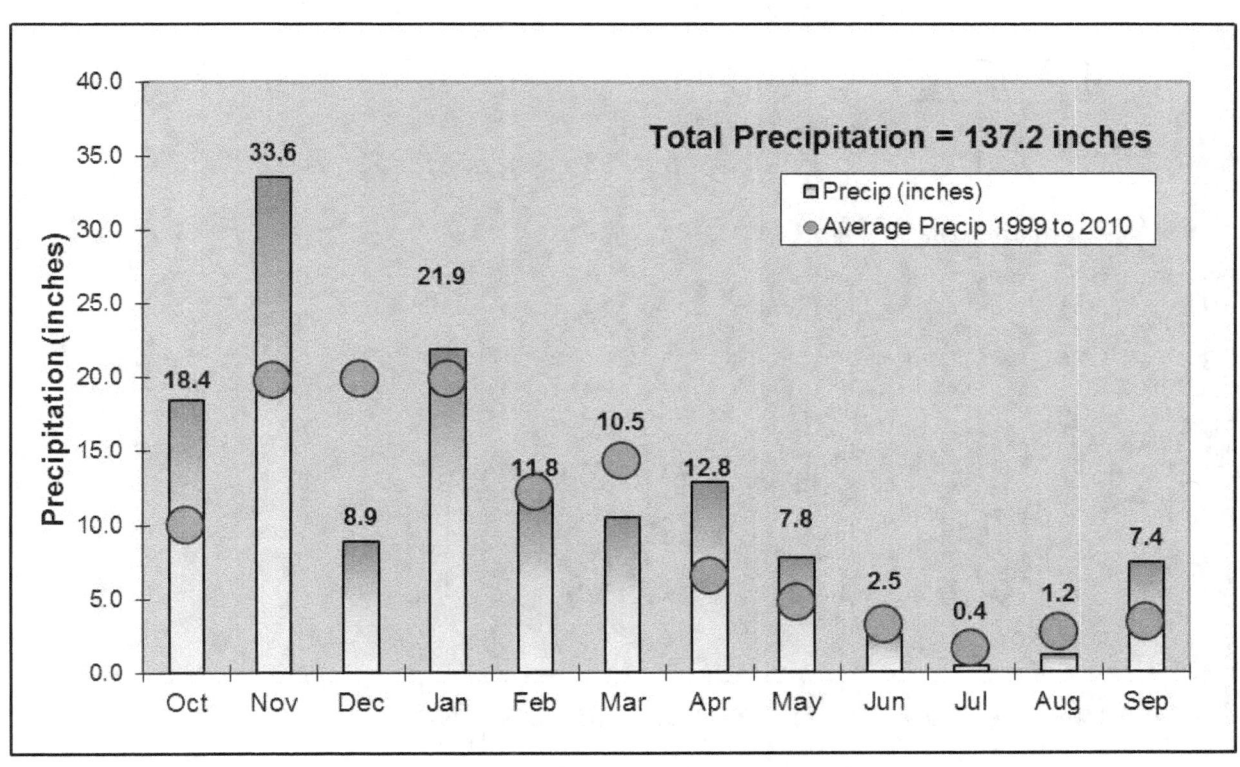

Figure H-3. Monthly precipitation values at the Quinault Rainforest, Water Year 2010 compared to the monthly averages for the period of record (1999-2010).

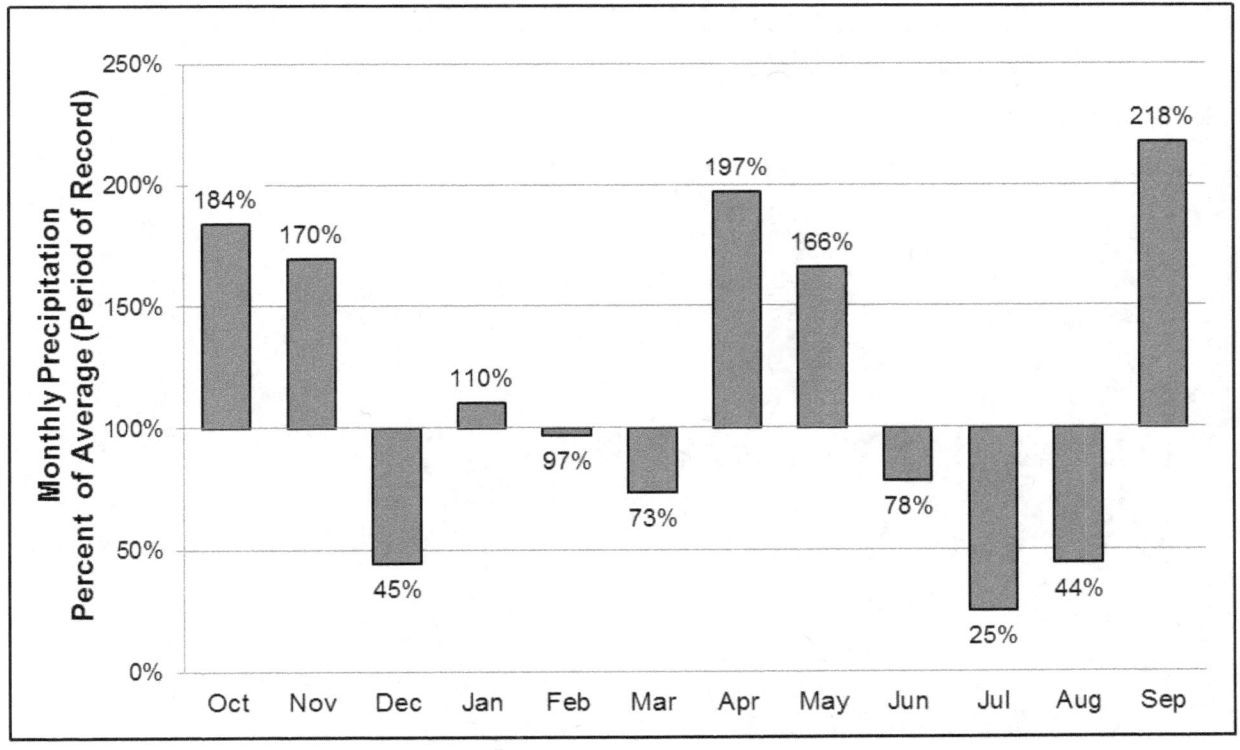

Figure H-4. Percent departure from the period of record (1999-2010) for precipitation at the Quinault Rainforest in Water Year 2010.

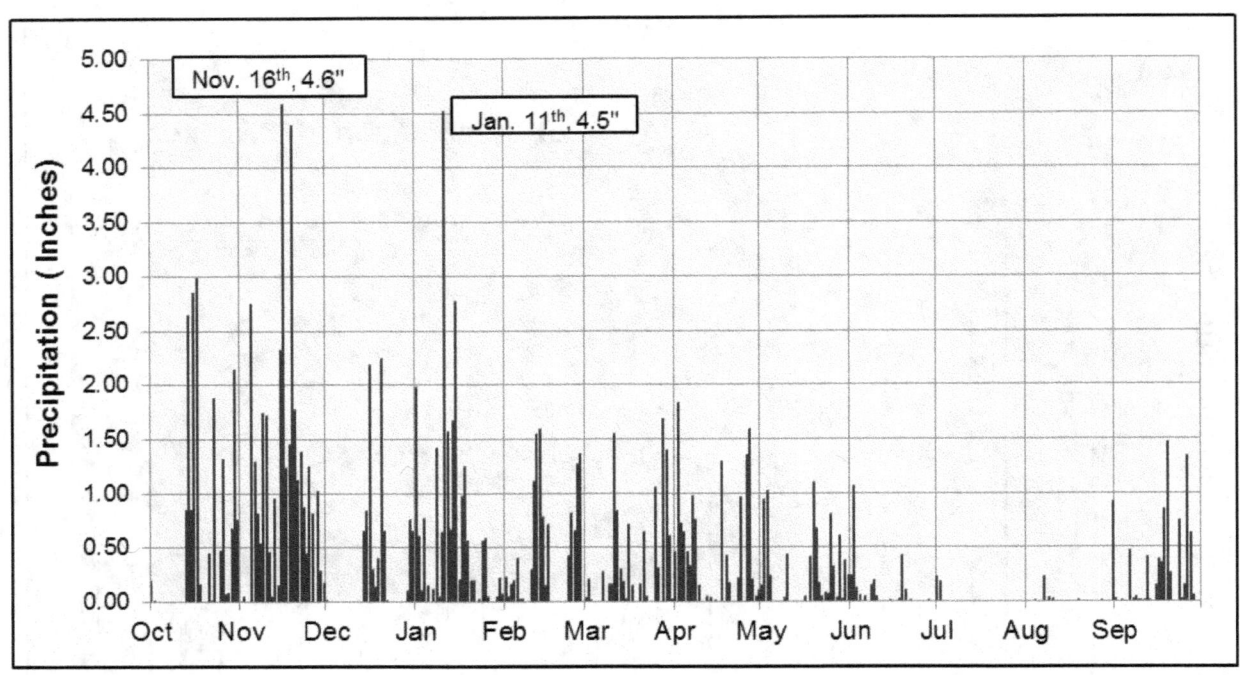

Figure H-5. Daily precipitation (inches) at the Quinault Rainforest, Water Year 2010.

Appendix I: Waterhole SNOTEL - Water Year 2010.

Temperatures ranged from an extreme low of -2.7°F on December 9, 2009 to a high of 75.7°F on July 9, 2010 (Table I-1). Late fall and early winter months were much colder than average (3.6°F below). Cold temperatures in November and December were replaced by warmer temperatures in January and February (1.2° above average) (Figure I-1). An extensive period of above freezing temperatures occurred in early January (Figure I-2). Spring returned to cooler than average temperatures (-1.7°), followed by a cooler than average summer (-1.3°) (Figure I-1).

The Waterhole SNOTEL received 86.2 inches of precipitation in Water Year 2010 (Figure I-3). Fall of 2009 was unusually wet with October and November combining at 176% of average (Figure I-4). Spring months were also wetter than average (157%). Summer months were generally drier than normal, especially the month of July. July 1 was followed by 41 days with little or no appreciable precipitation (Figure I-5). Dry conditions ended with a wetter than average September, with 3.1 inches of rainfall (191%) (Figure I-4).

Below average temperatures in fall, spring and summer months contributed to an above normal and long lasting mountain snowpack. Snowpack began developing on November 6, 2009 and melted out on July 8, 2010, persisting for 245 days. Maximum snow water equivalent was 54.0 inches on May 9, 2010 (Figure I-6). In late November, below average temperatures and above normal precipitation built a large snowpack and by December 1, 2009, the snowpack was 333% of average (Figure I-7). The snowpack neared the ten-year average during the dry and warmer months of mid-winter, before rebounding to well above average during the cold and snowy conditions of late spring (173% of average by June 1)(Figure I-7).

Table I-1. Monthly summary data, Waterhole SNOTEL, Water Year 2010.

Season	Month & Year	Mean Air Temp °F	Max Daily Air Temp °F	Min Daily Air Temp °F	Precipitation (inches)
Fall	October 2009	35.4	55.4	22.5	9.4
	November 2009	29.2	44.1	11.5	23.8
Winter	December 2009	24.0	44.8	-2.7	5.7
	January 2010	30.9	41.0	16.3	15.8
	February 2010	29.6	43.5	19.2	4.2
Spring	March 2010	29.1	50.4	10.8	8.8
	April 2010	28.8	52.7	14.2	7.5
	May 2010	34.6	55.6	15.1	6.2
Summer	June 2010	41.3	62.1	27.9	1.1
	July 2010	52.2	75.4	28.2	0.1
	August 2010	51.7	75.7	34.7	0.5
Fall	September 2010	45.4	66.2	32.7	3.1
Water Year Total		**36.0**	**75.7**	**-2.7**	**86.2**

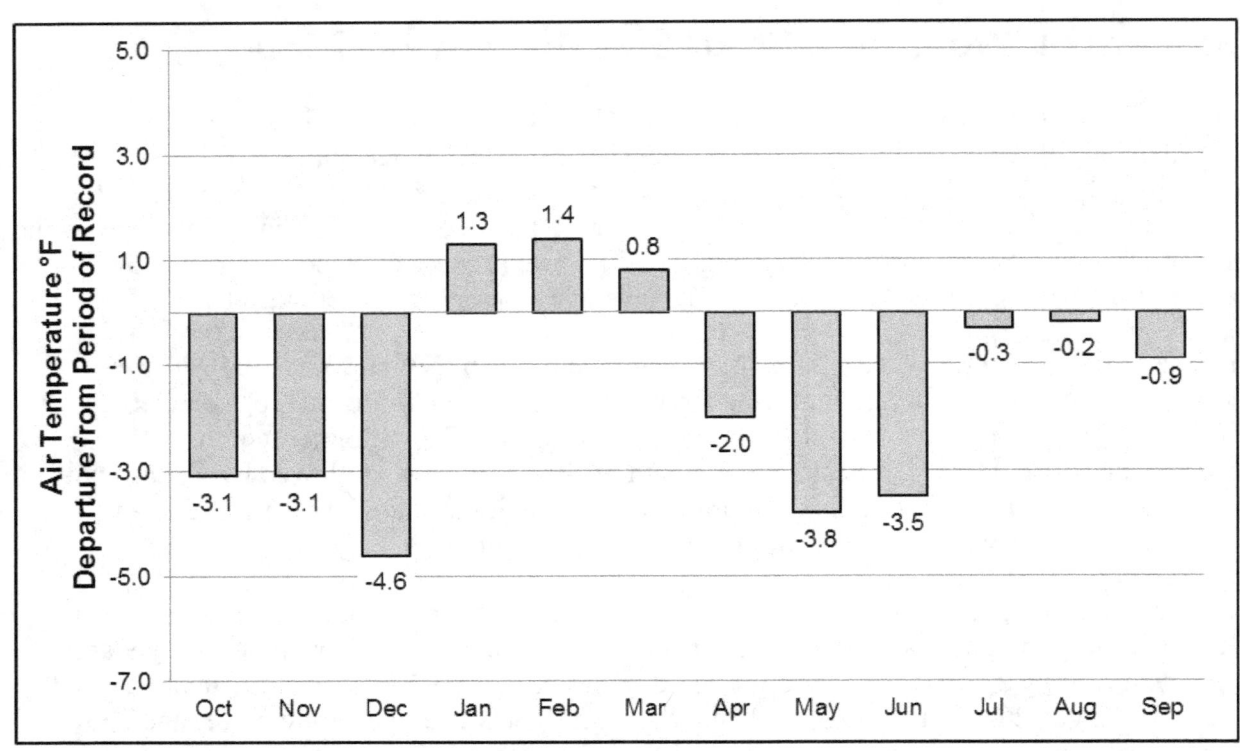

Figure I-1. Comparison of average monthly temperature (°F) for Waterhole SNOTEL in Water Year 2010 against monthly averages for the period of record (2000-2010).

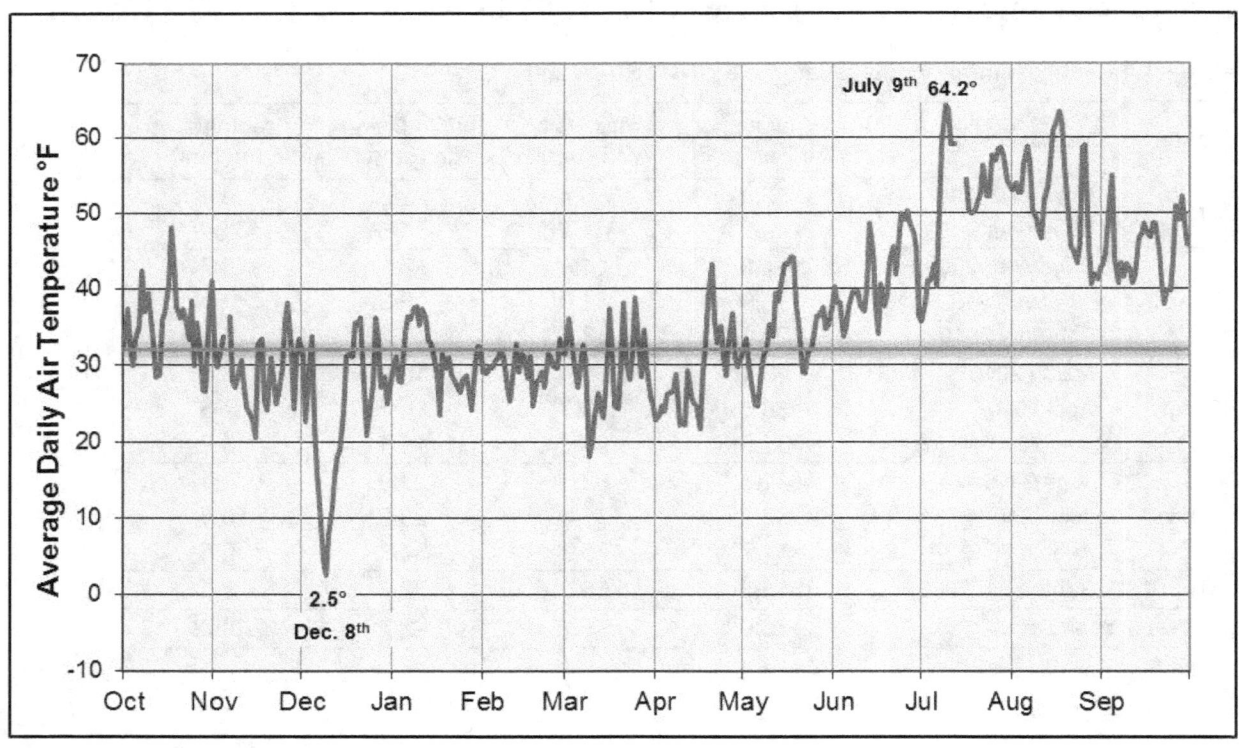

Figure I-2. Daily average air temp (°F) at the Waterhole SNOTEL, Water Year 2010. Blue line indicates 32°F, the freezing point of water.

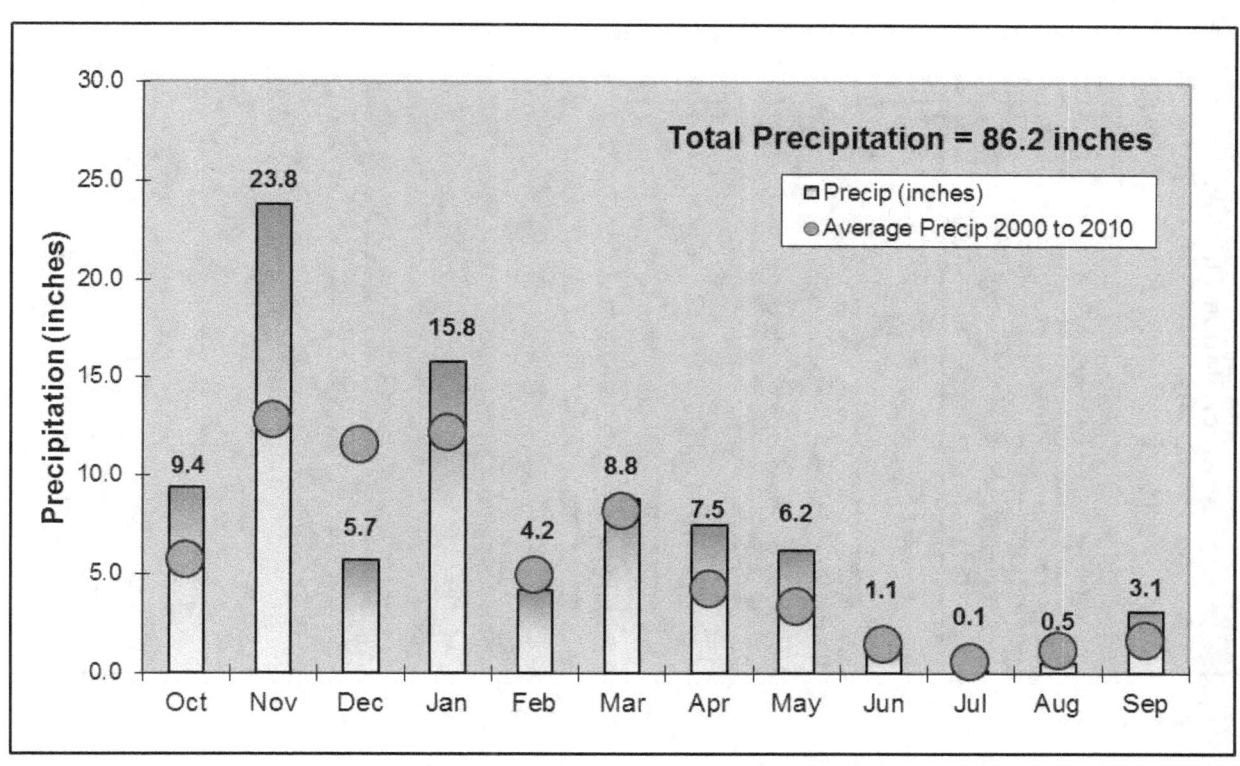

Figure I-3. Monthly precipitation values at the Waterhole SNOTEL, Water Year 2010 compared to the monthly averages for the period of record (2000-2010).

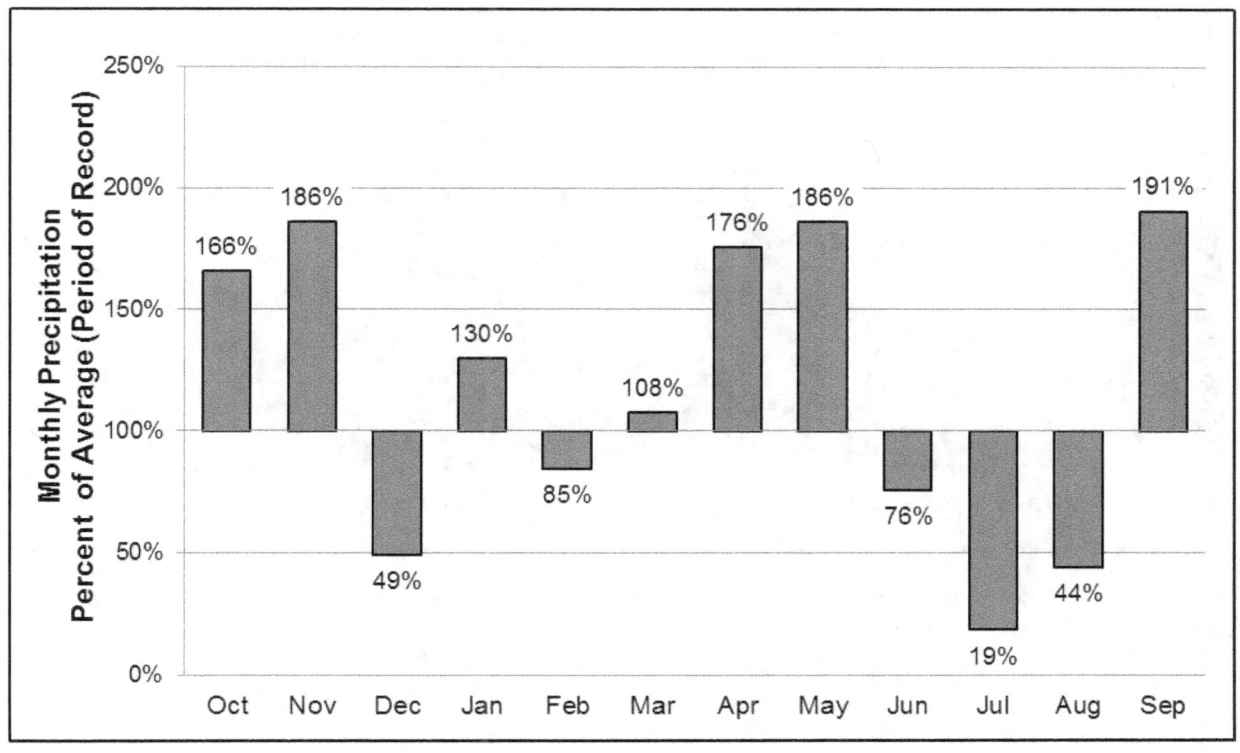

Figure I-4. Percent departure from the period of record (2000-2010) for precipitation at the Waterhole SNOTEL in Water Year 2010.

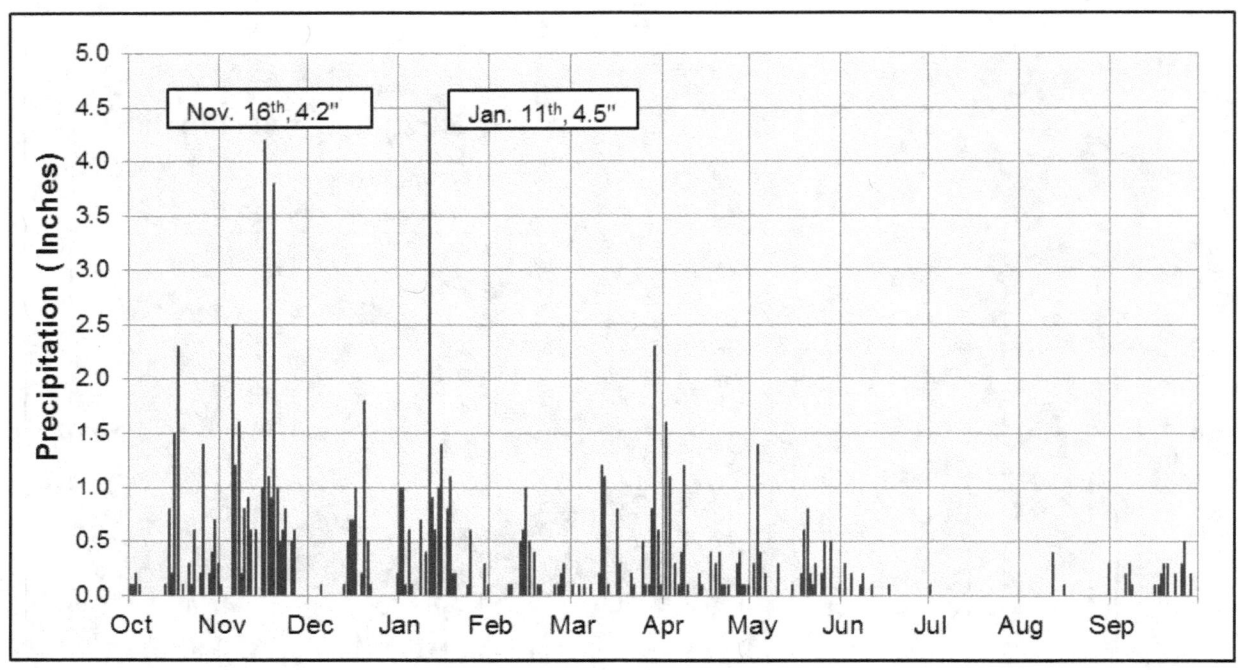

Figure I-5. Daily precipitation (inches) at the Waterhole SNOTEL, Water Year 2010.

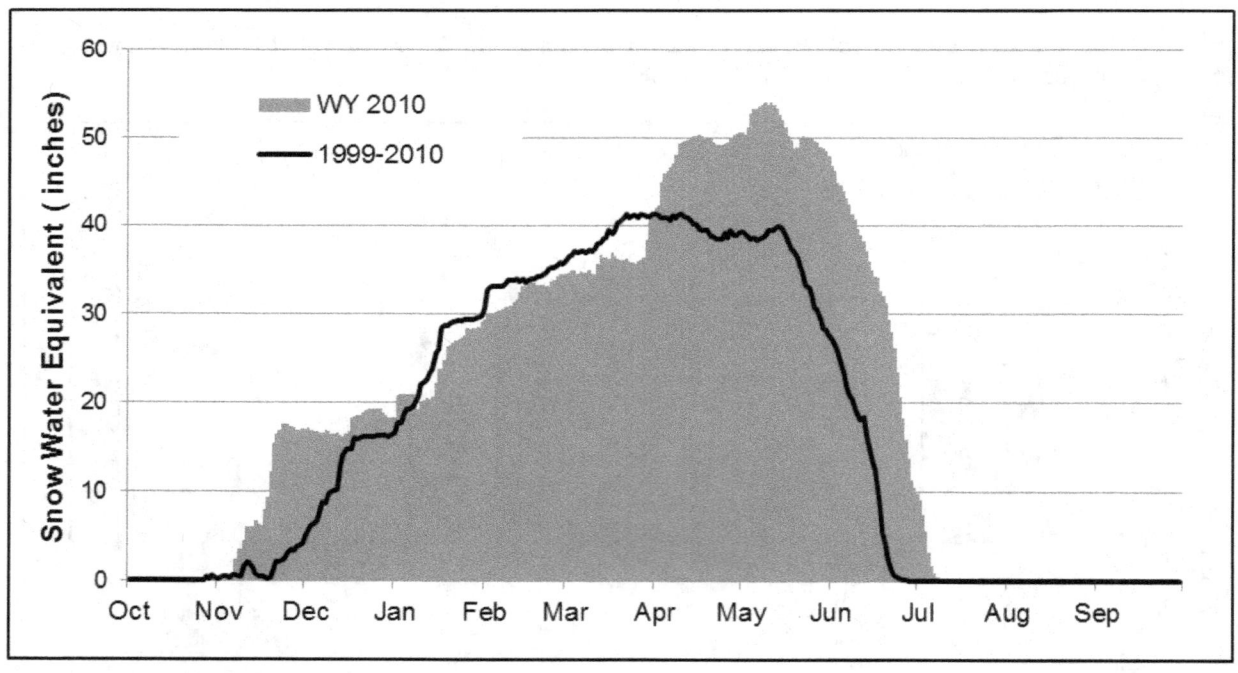

Figure I-6. Daily snow water equivalent (inches) at the Waterhole SNOTEL, Water Year 2010. The graph helps to illustrate the unusual early winter and late spring conditions. Well above average snow accumulations can be seen in mid-November and throughout the month of April.

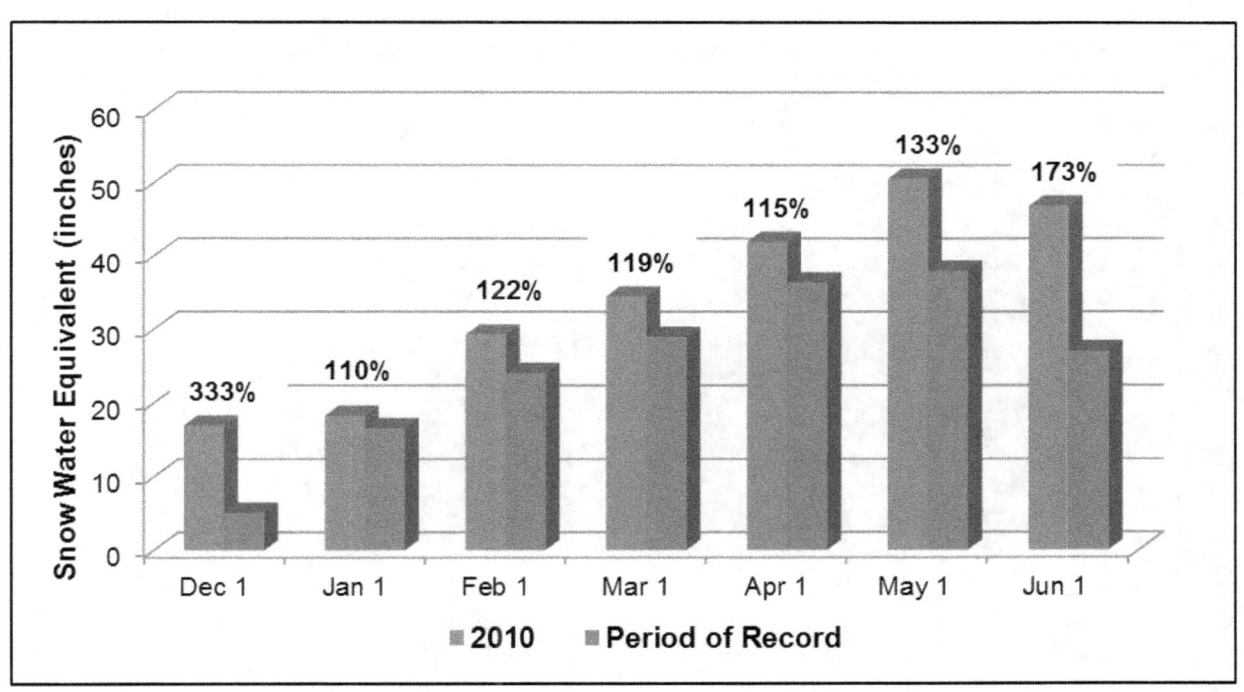

Figure I–7. First of the month snow water equivalent at the Waterhole SNOTEL in Water Year 2010, compared with the period of record (2000-2010).

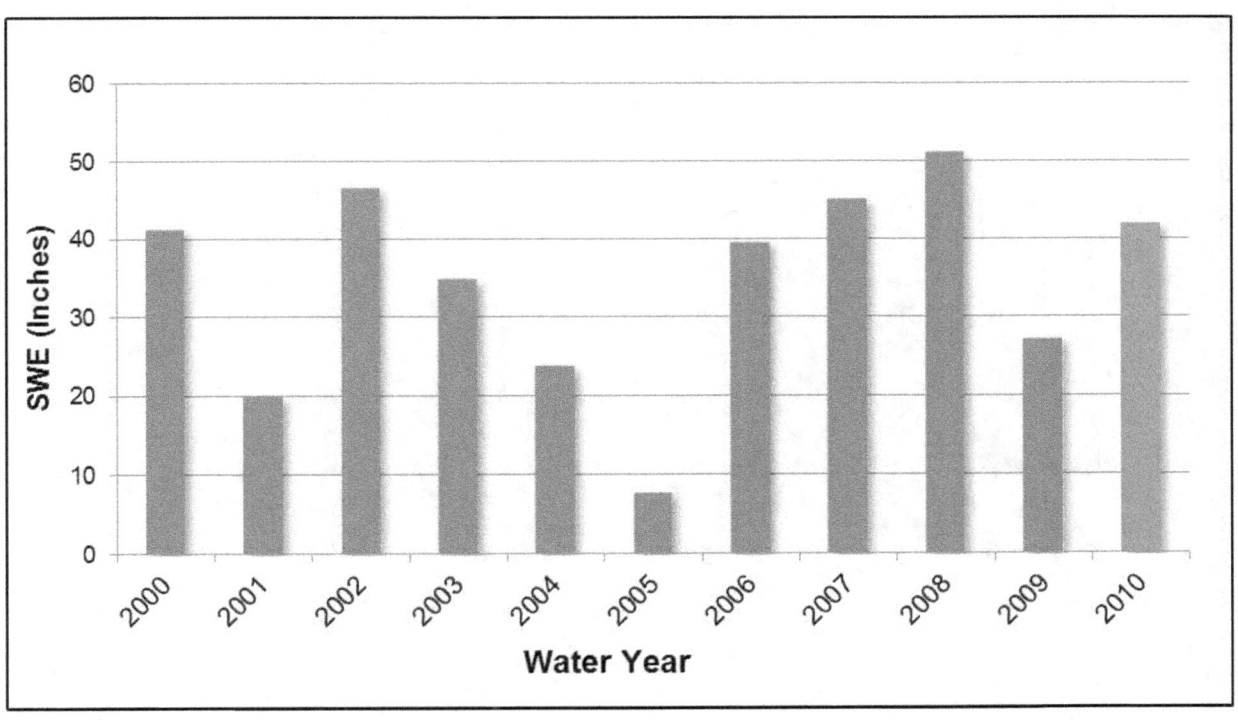

Figure I-8. April 1 snow water equivalent at the Waterhole SNOTEL for the period of record (2000 -2010). Highlighted column indicates Water Year 2010.